HOW THE BEATLES CHANGED THE WORLD

MARTIN W. SANDLER

WALKER BOOKS FOR YOUNG READERS
AN IMPRINT OF BLOOMSBURY
NEW YORK   LONDON   NEW DELHI   SYDNEY

This book is dedicated to Carol Sandler, who, like the Beatles,
has been a constant source of joy and enlightenment

First published in the United States of America in February 2014
by Walker Books for Young Readers, an imprint of Bloomsbury Publishing, Inc.
www.bloomsbury.com

For information about permission to reproduce selections from this book, write to
Permissions, Walker BFYR, 1385 Broadway, New York, New York 10018
Bloomsbury books may be purchased for business or promotional use. For information on bulk purchases please
contact Macmillan Corporate and Premium Sales Department at specialmarkets@macmillan.com

Library of Congress Cataloging-in-Publication Data
Sandler, Martin W.
How the Beatles changed the world / by Martin W. Sandler.
pages   cm
ISBN 978-0-8027-3565-2 (hardcover) • ISBN 978-0-8027-3566-9 (reinforced)
1. Beatles—Juvenile literature. 2. Rock musicians—England—Biography—Juvenile literature. I. Title.
ML3930.B39S26 2014   782.42166092'2—dc23   2013019876

Book design by Ellice Lee
Typeset in Janson
Printed in China by Leo Paper Products, Heshan, Guangdong
2 4 6 8 10 9 7 5 3 1 (hardcover)
2 4 6 8 10 9 7 5 3 1 (reinforced)

All papers used by Bloomsbury Publishing, Inc., are natural, recyclable products
made from wood grown in well-managed forests. The manufacturing processes
conform to the environmental regulations of the country of origin.

CONTENTS

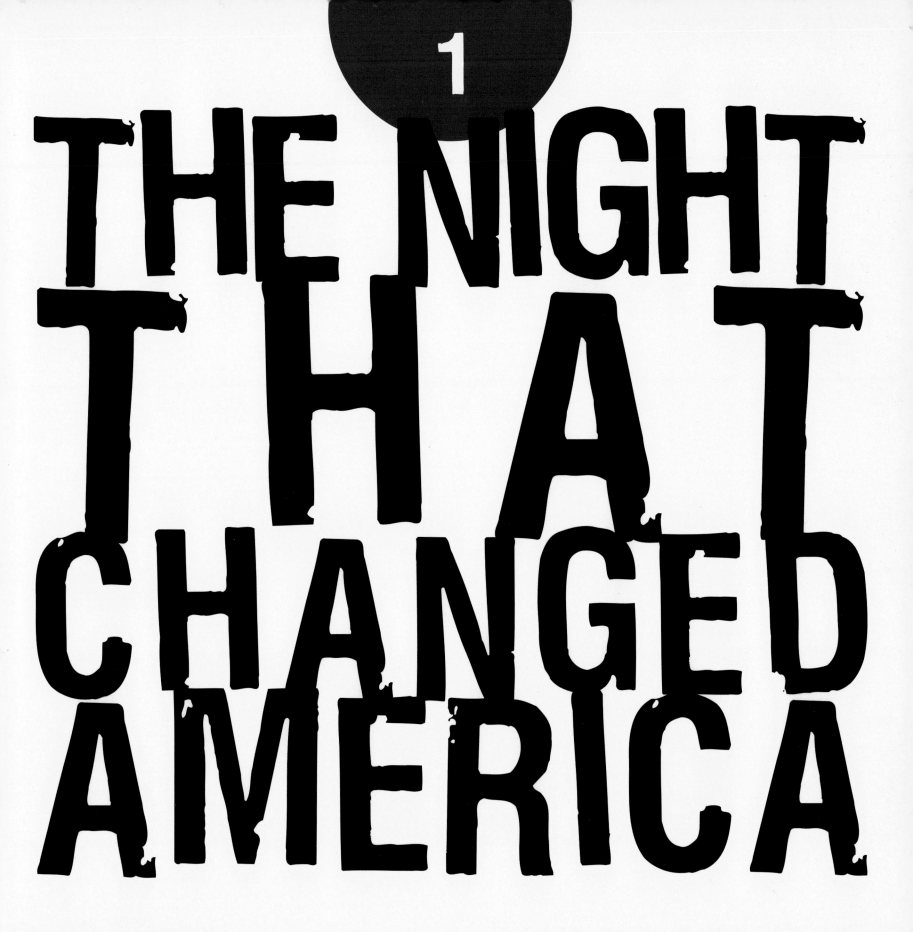

Police containing Beatles fans at Kennedy Airport

It was February 7, 1964, and the people of New York, America's

largest city, had never seen anything like it. The city's television stations were showing amazing live pictures of thousands of teenagers—mostly young girls—pouring into New York's Kennedy Airport. Other live pictures revealed an even more incredible sight. Thousands of teens, many of them screaming hysterically, a number of them fainting in anticipation, were pushing against police barricades that guarded the runways, waiting for a plane's arrival. Most adults watching the pictures had to wonder what was going on. Who was on that plane? Who in the world could be causing such a commotion?

New York's many radio stations were giving the answer. The plane was not carrying a beloved movie star or a legendary sports figure. Nor was it transporting one of the world's most important political leaders. Of all things, it was carrying a British rock-and-roll band with the strange name the Beatles on its first journey to America, where, on February 9, it was scheduled to perform on *The Ed Sullivan Show*, the nation's most popular television program.

Most American parents may not have known who the Beatles were, but hundreds of thousands of their children did. Thanks to radio disc jockeys across the nation, they had learned that four young pop musicians from Liverpool named John Lennon, Paul McCartney, George Harrison, and Ringo Starr, who called themselves the Beatles, had taken all of England by storm. Radio stations had been playing one of the Beatles' songs, "I Want to Hold Your Hand," over and over again, and the kids had fallen in love with it. In fact, they had rushed out to the record stores and made it the number-one song in America—the first time a song topped the pop charts in both the United States and the United Kingdom simultaneously.

Screaming teenagers wave a sign as they welcome the Beatles.

In an unprecedented maneuver, radio stations had actually begun reporting on the plane carrying the Beatles from the moment it had taken off from England. "It is now 6:30 a.m. Beatle time," one station reported. "They left London thirty minutes ago. They're out over the Atlantic Ocean, headed for New York. The temperature is 32 Beatle degrees." Reports of the plane's progress continued throughout the flight. And they were not the only announcements being made. Every fifteen minutes, New York's top two radio stations made it known that every fan who went out to the airport to greet the plane's arrival would be given a free Beatles T-shirt.

By the time the aircraft touched down at the airport, pure pandemonium had broken out. Even the most veteran policemen and reporters were stunned. "We've never seen anything like this here before," an airport official exclaimed. "Never. Not even for kings and queens." One security officer put it simply. "I think," he declared, "the world has gone mad."

Finally, the airplane landed. As its wheels touched down, the four young Beatles were filled with their own emotions. They had absolutely no idea of what awaited them. George was the only member of the group who had ever been to the United States. "They've got everything over there," he later recalled thinking.

"What do they want us for?" Ringo had his doubts as well. "Going to the States was a big step,"

he would later remember. "People said just because we were popular in Britain, why should we be there?"

It was a genuine concern. All four Beatles were very aware of what had happened to one of their idols, Cliff Richard. One of England's greatest pop stars, Richard had gone to America intent on making a big name for himself there as well. And he had failed. So too had other British musical entertainers.

The Beatles got their first hint that things might turn out differently for them as soon as the aircraft's doors were thrown open. At once, they were greeted by a roar, the volume of which they had never heard, even during their most spectacular triumphs in England. The thousands of young people who had waited for the doors to open had their own reaction. Their new idols were young, they were handsome, and they were smiling and waving at them. But that was not what struck them most about the Beatles. It was their hair. It came down over their ears and was bowl-shaped, so different from anything they had ever seen. And these new American fans loved the look of it.

The pandemonium increased as the Beatles started down the aircraft's steps. Photographers, perched precariously in a basket attached to a hydraulic crane, appeared next to the plane, begging the startled Beatles to halt their descent and pose for pictures. At the same time, reporters raced toward the steps shouting out questions even before reaching them.

As soon as they managed to make their way down the stairs, the Beatles were hustled into a terminal-building conference room where they were to hold their first press conference in America. When they stepped into the room, they were as startled by the bedlam they encountered as they had been when they had first stepped off their plane. It was a mob scene. More than two hundred reporters from newspapers and magazines around the world were shouting questions all at once. Flashbulbs from photographers' cameras were going off like strobe lights. In the back of the room, two girls, who had managed to sneak in, fainted at the sight of the four young rock and rollers.

The Beatles (left to right: John, George, Paul, and Ringo) were amazed by their American welcome.

Finally the room was somehow quieted down and the press conference began. It took only a few minutes for the American press to discover what the British media had already learned. Each of the Beatles was as funny and quick-witted as he was musically talented. Asked, "How do you find America?" Ringo replied, "Turn left at Greenland." Asked if they hoped to take anything home with them, they answered, "The Rockefeller Center." After a score of other quick and playful responses to the reporters' barrage of questions, Paul ended the press conference by putting on his most serious face. "We have a message," he announced. For the first time, the room grew silent as all waited for his profound statement. "Our message is," he proclaimed, "buy more Beatles records!"

Having delighted the press, the Beatles, surrounded by some of New York's burliest policemen, were escorted out the terminal's rear entrance to where four chauffeur-driven limousines were waiting to take them to the Plaza Hotel. Paul did not make the short trip unscathed. Just as he reached the cars, a photographer, determined to obtain a scoop by discovering whether the Beatles were wearing wigs, grabbed a handful of his hair and pulled it hard. By this time, a huge mob of young fans had discovered just where the band was making its escape. As the Beatles came racing toward the cars, policemen literally picked each of them up and threw them into the vehicles, while an officer shouted to one of the drivers, "Get out of here, buddy, if you want to get out alive."

It was a frightening experience. But for the Beatles, each of whom had had serious doubts about how successful they might be in America, fear was overshadowed by an overwhelming realization. "We thought, 'Wow!... We have really made it!'" Paul would later recall. "I remember, for instance, the great moment of getting into the limo and putting on the radio, and hearing a running commentary on us: 'They have just left the airport and are coming towards New York City . . .' It was like a dream. The greatest fantasy ever."

The Beatles would spend the next two days at the Plaza Hotel, under heavy guard from the thousands of fans who now surrounded the building, chanting, "*We want the Beatles!*" Meanwhile, CBS Studio 50, from which *The Ed Sullivan Show* was broadcast, was having its own problems. The studio could accommodate an audience of seven hundred. Already, more than fifty thousand requests for tickets had come pouring in.

What very few people knew was that there was an even bigger problem. George had come down with a throat infection. An examination by the hotel's doctor revealed that he had a temperature of 104 degrees. As a performance that had captured the attention of almost all America was fast approaching, one of the Beatles was in danger of not even being able to appear.

The Beatles were scheduled to rehearse twice in the days leading up to *The Ed Sullivan Show* telecast. Saturday afternoon they would conduct a walk-through, which meant the band would lip-synch its performance so that the camera and lighting crews could set themselves up in the best possible positions for the actual broadcast. With George remaining in his hotel room resting and receiving medication, the Beatles' road manager, Neil Aspinall, substituted for him. "I stood in for [George]," Aspinall would later explain, "so that they could mark where everyone

Paul McCartney gives Ed Sullivan a guitar lesson.

would stand, and I had a guitar strapped round me. It wasn't plugged in—nobody was playing anything—and it was amazing to read in a major American magazine a few days later that I 'played a mean guitar.'"

At the end of the walk-through, Ed Sullivan had jokingly said that if George was unable to perform on the telecast Sunday night, he would put on a Beatles wig and take his place. Fortunately, by Sunday morning George was feeling much better and announced himself ready to perform not only on the telecast but at the rehearsal scheduled for that afternoon.

By the time that rehearsal was ready to begin, the theater was surrounded by thousands of young Beatles fans. It had been decided that the rehearsal would be conducted before a live audience. But given the limited number of seats in the theater and the far greater number of teenagers frantic to attend the dress rehearsal, it was inevitable that there would be chaos even before the actual program. As one of Ed Sullivan's assistants would later recall, "On the day of the broadcast . . . there was complete pandemonium. Mass hysteria. I don't think the Beatles believed what was happening. No one believed it."

Another thing that the Beatles had not anticipated was just how long a day that Sunday, February 9, 1964, was going to be. "The main thing I was aware of when we did the first *Ed Sullivan Show*," Ringo would later recount, "was that we rehearsed all afternoon." It had indeed been exhausting, and yet they still could not relax before the broadcast, which was now only a few hours away. According to the deal their manager had made with Sullivan, they still had to tape two performances that would be shown on future shows once the band was back in England.

When the taping was completed, they were hustled back to the Plaza for a couple of hours' rest. Almost before they knew it, it was time to return to the theater. A night that would change America was about to begin.

The program started with Ed Sullivan informing his audience that a telegram had been received from the most famous of all rock-and-roll stars, Elvis Presley, and his manager,

The Beatles rehearse for *The Ed Sullivan Show.*

congratulating the group on its *Sullivan Show* appearance and its visit to America. Actually the Beatles had been handed the telegram half an hour before the program began. After reading it, George, in typical Beatles deadpan fashion, had asked, "Elvis who?"

After reminding his viewers that *The Ed Sullivan Show* had occasioned many exciting nights featuring some of the world's greatest entertainers, Sullivan exclaimed, "Now tonight the whole country is waiting to hear England's Beatles, and you're gonna hear them, and they're tremendous ambassadors of good will." Having teased the frenzied audience in the studio and the millions in front of their TV sets at home, Sullivan paused for a commercial. Once it was over, he launched into an even longer introduction to the band everyone was still waiting to see and hear.

"Now yesterday and today," Sullivan stated, "our theater's been jammed with newspapermen and hundreds of photographers from all over the nation, and these veterans agreed with me that the city never has witnessed the excitement stirred by these youngsters from Liverpool, who call themselves the Beatles. Let's bring them on."

Sullivan's last few words were drowned out by the screams of the teenagers in the audience as John, Paul, George, and Ringo at last appeared on the stage. The screeching got even louder as the Beatles launched into their song "All My Loving." As the teenagers shouted and bounced in their seats, Paul then took the spotlight, singing "Till There Was You," the hit song from the popular Broadway musical *The Music Man.* During this song, for the benefit of the millions of viewers at home, the camera cut to each of the Beatles and identified him by putting his first name on the screen.

When the camera focused on John, the caption also read "SORRY GIRLS, HE'S MARRIED."

The group concluded their first segment by singing another of their own songs, "She Loves You."

After the customary commercials, the Beatles' opening segment was followed by a series of acts typical of an *Ed Sullivan Show.* First up was a magician named Fred Kaps, who performed a number of sleight-of-hand tricks. During the dress rehearsal the day before, Sullivan had told the teenagers who had tickets for the live program that they could scream all they wanted for the Beatles as long as they were quiet during the other acts. He had jokingly warned that if they didn't comply, he'd "send for a barber" to trim the Beatles' hair.

Impatient as they were for the Beatles' return, the young fans remained quiet during the magician's performance and the other acts that followed. They included the cast of the Broadway show *Oliver!* (featuring a young man named Davy Jones, who would go on to be the popular lead singer for the Monkees), the impressionist Frank Gorshin (who would later become more famous by playing the Riddler on the *Batman* television series), the singer Tessie O'Shea, and a comedy team called McCall & Brill.

Then it was time for the main attraction to return. As the audience's screaming and screeching resumed, the Beatles concluded their performance with "I Saw Her Standing There" and their megahit "I Want to Hold Your Hand."

When they finished, Paul, John, and George put down their instruments. Ringo jumped down from the drum platform. Then they all went over to Ed Sullivan, shook his hand, and waved to the now-hysterical audience. After they left the stage, Sullivan made an announcement unlike any he had ever made on his program. "All of us on the show," he declared, "want to express our deep appreciation to the New York Police Department for its superb handling of thousands of youngsters who cluttered Broadway at 53rd Street ready to greet the Beatles . . . and our deep appreciation to the newspapermen, magazine writers, and photographers who have been so darn kind to the Beatles and us."

It was an announcement only the Beatles could have inspired. But it was far from the most extraordinary thing to come out of the group's *Ed Sullivan Show* appearance.

When the viewing figures were tallied, they were not only record shattering but almost unbelievable.

Seventy-three million people had watched the Beatles on television that one night—the largest TV audience for an entertainment program—ever! The show was watched in more than twenty-three million American homes.

It was also revealed that while the program was being aired, much of the nation had come to a standstill. It was almost impossible to get a bus or a taxi anywhere. Even more amazing was the fact that from 8:00 p.m. to 9:00 p.m. that Sunday, crime rates in many American cities fell to an all-time low. Even the criminals were glued to their television sets, watching the Beatles.

For weeks after the program was over, the Beatles' appearance was among the hottest topics of conversation. Many in both the news and entertainment industries were astounded by what had taken place. "I was amazed," America's leading news anchor, Walter Cronkite, would exclaim, "that these figures on the stage could generate such hysteria." One of England's top theatrical agents was equally astounded. "I never believed when Ed booked the Beatles that it would be so big . . . ," he confessed. "By the time the show went on the air, it became a piece of theatrical history."

As far as the Beatles themselves were concerned, each of them had his own opinion about their introduction to America. "We had no idea of what *The Ed Sullivan Show* meant," Ringo would later state. "We didn't know how huge it was. I don't think we were nervous because we were doing songs that we knew how to play, we'd done them before and we'd done plenty of TV. But the idea of just coming to America was the mind-blower—no one can imagine these days what an incredible feat it was to conquer America. No British act had done it before. We were just coming over to do our stuff, hopefully get recognized and to sell some records. But it turned into something huge."

Much later, Paul would give his own assessment of what

the *Ed Sullivan Show* appearance meant not only to the Beatles, but to those who watched the program. "It was very important," he would declare. "We came out of nowhere with funny hair . . . That was very influential. I think that was really one of the big things that [made] us—the hairdo more than the music, originally. A lot of people's fathers had wanted to turn us off . . . but a lot of mothers and children made them keep it on. All these kids are now grown-up, and telling us they remember it. . . . I get people . . . saying, 'Oh man, I remember that Sunday night; we didn't know what had hit us—just sitting there watching Ed Sullivan's show.' Up until then there were jugglers and comedians . . . and then, suddenly, the Beatles!"

Interestingly enough, many who watched the show that night did not understand what had hit them. For instance, *Newsweek* magazine's entertainment critic wrote, "The big question in the music business at the moment is: will the Beatles last . . . ? The odds are that they will fade

Ed Sullivan changed the Beatles' lives.

away, as most adults confidently predict." His opinion was shared by Ed Sullivan's own musical director, Ray Block: ". . . as far as I can see," he declared, "I give them a year."

They could not have been more wrong. Nor could they have more seriously misjudged the extraordinary impact of the Beatles' appearance on *The Ed Sullivan Show*. Coming at a time when the nation still mourned the assassination of its popular president John F. Kennedy only three months before, the sensation caused by the fun-loving, upbeat Beatles provided some sunny relief. Today, fifty years later, those who watched the program remember it as vividly

Left to right: the Kennedy Assassination, the first moon landing, the September 11th attack

as they remember where they were when Kennedy was killed, when man first stepped on the moon, or when the terrible tragedy that was 9/11 took place.

And with good reason. For as one Beatles chronicler has stated, "When the Beatles made their first appearance on *The Ed Sullivan Show* that February 1964, it was and remains the most important event in the history of rock music." The Ed Sullivan website has put it this way: "The genius of the Beatles and the American institution that was *The Ed Sullivan Show* combined to create one of the most defining and indelible moments in the history of music, television and pop culture. It was a remarkable convergence that came at a special time in America, making an impact on the world that will never be duplicated."

Even those individuals who, prior to the historic telecast, had refused to take the Beatles seriously would change their tune. Among them was Jack Paar, the host of the highly popular late night *Jack Paar Program*. He admitted he had regarded the Beatles and all the hysteria that surrounded them "as a joke." "I didn't know," he would later confess, "they were going to change the culture of the country with music."

2

HOW THE BEATLES CHANGED POPULAR MUSIC

Elvis was the King of Rock and Roll.

The impact of the Beatles' appearance

on that February 9, 1964, evening went well beyond the amazing number of people who watched the show. It transcended the fact that more than half of America was brought to a standstill by four mop-topped young men from Liverpool. The Beatles were not only about to become the most successful musical group in history; they were about to change the popular culture of the nation.

The Beatles were certainly not the first rock-and-roll performers to have gained attention. There was Buddy Holly and the Crickets, Bill Haley and the Comets, Little Richard, and, up to that moment, the king of them all, Elvis Presley. But the Beatles were different. Until then, all rock-and-roll groups were really solo acts. They featured a main performer backed up by other rock musicians. The Beatles had no feature performer. They performed totally as a group. It was an enormous change, one that would dramatically alter how popular music was presented.

The unprecedented popularity the Beatles achieved would bring about another dramatic change as well. Before John, Paul, George, and Ringo arrived in America, the only rock-and-roll groups to make it big in the United States were Americans. The sensation the Beatles caused through their *Ed Sullivan Show* appearance led directly to what became known as the British Invasion, making it possible for British groups such as the Animals, Herman's Hermits, the Searchers, the Dave Clark Five, and Gerry and the Pacemakers to achieve American success.

Herman's Hermits

And there was much more. The Beatles changed the very nature of the recording known as a single. Before CDs and MP3s, most hit songs were bought as a small record that had an A and a B side. The A side of a single contained the song expected to be a hit, and the B side contained a song of less importance. The Beatles forever altered the world of the single by having both the A side and the B side of their records play a song they felt was of the highest standard. This practice was never more clearly seen than on their hit record with "Penny Lane" on one side and "Strawberry Fields Forever" on the other. Top rock bands such as the Rolling Stones would later follow suit.

During their days together, the Beatles compiled an amazing total of number-one singles. Because until 1969 there was more than one singles chart that people paid attention to, the exact number of their number-one singles varied. All the charts indicate that the Beatles had seventeen number ones in Great Britain. Their

A record player and hit singles

total number ones in the United States varies from twenty to twenty-seven, depending on which charts are consulted. Had they concentrated solely on producing these hit singles, they still would have been the greatest pop-music recording artists of all time. But in the ways they redefined the record album, they made one of their greatest contributions to changing the world of popular music. Prior to the Beatles, albums were not as important as singles. They commonly contained one or two songs that had already been hits. The rest of the songs were included to fill out the album. The Beatles gave new meaning and new importance to the album by creating it to include all hit or potential hit songs.

Also revolutionary was the way in which the Beatles created albums that included not simply a series of unrelated songs but songs built around a central theme. The inclusion of orchestral instruments and sound effects in certain songs was groundbreaking too.

And that was not all. Generations of Beatles fans have proclaimed that one of the things they enjoy most about the band's work is the way the Beatles revolutionized the album cover. It began with the album *With the Beatles* (UK album title of *Meet the Beatles!*).

"That cover," George would state, "was the beginning of us being actively involved in the Beatles' artwork.

The [earlier] *Please Please Me* album cover is [awful], but at that time it hadn't mattered. We hadn't even thought it was lousy, probably because we were so pleased to be on a record. *With the Beatles* was the first one where we thought, 'Hey, let's get artistic.'" And they did. And because of them, album covers would never be the same.

These were all revolutionary and enduring changes. But they were not the most important ways in which, as author Jonathan Gould has written, "The Beatles changed the way people listened to popular music and experienced its role in their lives." The Beatles' greatest contribution by far lies in their music and their lyrics. Before them, most rock-and-roll performers sang songs written by professional songwriters. The Beatles set the stage for what became the common practice of rock-and-roll performers' writing their own songs. Aside from some notable contributions by George, the majority would be written by John and Paul, two young men who had received a far better education than almost all other rock and rollers. Their interest in art and literature would not only set them apart from other pop-music performers, but would influence many of the songs they would come to write.

There were many other factors that would lead to the success of their extraordinary collaboration. Personally, they were two very different people. Paul was cheerful and optimistic. John was serious, often intense. It was a combination that allowed for each to make up for what the other lacked. They worked together in a very special way. Sometimes, each would write a song himself. More often, one of them would write half a song and the other would complete it. It was this process that led to a productive rivalry, one in which each tried to outdo the other.

One of the things they shared, particularly in their earlier days together, was their ability to write a song

Though they dressed alike, Paul's (left) and John's (right) personalities were very different, resulting in a songwriting partnership that was unparalleled.

that made each of their young female fans feel that the song was directed at her. It was no accident that many of the early songs that John and Paul wrote had the word "you" in the title—for example, "From Me to You," "Thank You Girl," and "I Want to Hold Your Hand."

The ways in which John and Paul's songwriting became increasingly sophisticated were also revolutionary. They never lost sight of the importance of finding the most perfect title for their compositions. "John and I were always looking for titles," Paul would recall.

> "Once you've got a good title, if someone says 'What's your new song?' and you have a title that interests people, you are halfway there.

Of course, the song has to be good. If you've called it 'I Am on My Way to a Party with You, Babe,' they might say OK . . . But if you've called it 'Eight Days a Week,' they say, 'Oh yes, that's good!' With 'A Hard Day's Night,' you've almost captured them."

John and Paul shared another vital songwriting attribute as well. They each had the ability to find inspiration in almost everything around them.

One of the most popular of all Beatles songs was actually occasioned by a marital breakup. In 1968, John and his wife, Cynthia, were about to get divorced. Paul was very close to their five-year-old son, Julian. Wishing to show his support for Cynthia and Julian, he drove to their home to speak with them. Paul often began thinking of new songs while driving, and during the one-hour trip, he started singing the words "Hey Jools" accompanied by words to comfort him.

As Paul would later recount, "John and Cynthia were splitting up and I felt particularly sorry for Julian. I had known them for so long . . . I thought, as a friend of the family, I would motor out . . . and tell them that everything was all right: to try and cheer them up, basically, and see how they were. I had about an hour's drive. I would always turn the radio off and try and make up songs, just in case . . . I started singing: 'Hey Jools—don't make it bad, take a sad song, and make it better . . .' It was optimistic, a hopeful message for Julian: 'Come on, man, your parents got divorced. I know you're not happy, but you'll be OK.' I eventually changed 'Jools' to 'Jude.' One of the characters in [a musical show I liked called *Oklahoma!*] is called Jud, and I [liked] the name."

When John finished adding his contribution to the song, "Hey Jude" was the longest of all Beatles songs. It was so long (some seven minutes) that George Martin, who was producing its recording, was concerned. "After I timed it," Martin later recalled, "I actually said, 'You can't make a single that long.' I was shouted down by the boys—not for the first time in my life—and John asked, 'Why not?' I couldn't think of a good answer, really—except the pathetic one that disc jockeys wouldn't play it. He said, 'They will if it's us.' And, of course, he was absolutely right."

Amazing as it seems, the music for the Beatles' greatest hit song and one of the most successful pop songs of all time came to one member of the group while he was sleeping. When Paul woke up one morning, the tune for what would become "Yesterday" was running through his head. He had a piano by his bed and immediately started playing it. "It was just all there," he later stated. "A complete thing. I couldn't believe it."

The tune was, in fact, so complete that Paul feared it must have come from a song written by someone else that he had dredged up from his memory. "For about a month," he said, "I went round to people in the music business and asked them whether they had ever heard it before." When it became clear that he had not unconsciously "borrowed" the tune, he began to write words to the music.

Anxious to set down words that fit the tune, he came up with the first words he thought of. For whatever reason, they had to do with scrambled eggs. "Scrambled eggs, oh my baby, how I love your legs . . . I believe in scrambled eggs," Paul recalled writing. "Over the next couple of weeks I started to put in the [real] words. I liked the tune and I thought I'd like to take some

Paul with John's son Julian

time over the words, get something that fitted like 'scrambled eggs.' And then, one day, I had the idea of 'Yesterday.'"

When Paul finished writing lyrics that pleased him, he took the song to the rest of the group. "I brought the song into the studio for the first time and played it on the guitar," he recalled, "but soon Ringo said, 'I can't really put any drums on—it wouldn't make sense.' And John and George said, 'There's no point in having another guitar.' So George Martin suggested, 'Why don't you just try it yourself and see how it works.'"

Paul not only tried it, it became his most successful song. "It's amazing," he would state, "that it just came to me in a dream." "Yesterday," the song that began with a dream and "scrambled eggs," is today the most recorded song in history, with over 3,000 versions of it having been recorded by various artists. It has been played on the radio more times than any song ever written.

Undoubtedly, John and Paul's greatest accomplishment as songwriters was that they never stopped growing. They started by creating songs that were catchy and appealing but not particularly profound. By the time the band broke up, they had written words and melodies whose messages inspired millions of people throughout the world and changed their lives. No wonder the music critic for London's *Sunday Times* would declare John and Paul to be the "greatest composers since Beethoven." It was an astounding, unprecedented accomplishment. And it was even more extraordinary because of the way the Beatles began.

ALL YOU NEED IS LOVE

Perhaps the greatest impact of the Beatles' songs came from the inspirational messages contained in so many of their lyrics. Nothing had greater impact than the message of love they continually conveyed, particularly to young people. And nothing gave them a better opportunity to spread that message to a greater number of people than the first worldwide telecast on June 25, 1967.

At the beginning of that year, the Beatles were asked by the British Broadcasting Corporation (BBC) to contribute a song simple enough to be understood by viewers of all nationalities.

Although both Paul and John began separately working on a song for the show, it was decided that John's composition titled "All You Need Is Love" was perfect for the telecast. As Paul would later state, "'All You Need Is Love' was John's song. I threw in a few ideas, as did the other members of the group. . . ." Brian Epstein was particularly taken with the result. "The nice thing about it is that it cannot be misinterpreted. It is a clear message saying that love is everything."

When it aired, the program was watched by more than four hundred million people in approximately twenty-five countries. As Ringo would later state, "We were big enough to command an audience of that size, and it was for love. . . . peace and love, people putting flowers in guns."

Commenting on "All You Need Is Love," which went quickly to number one on the bestselling record charts, Neil Aspinall stated, "It expressed the mood of the times, with Flower Power and all that whole movement." And it would be the Beatles, more than anyone else, who would spread the message around the world.

Flower power.

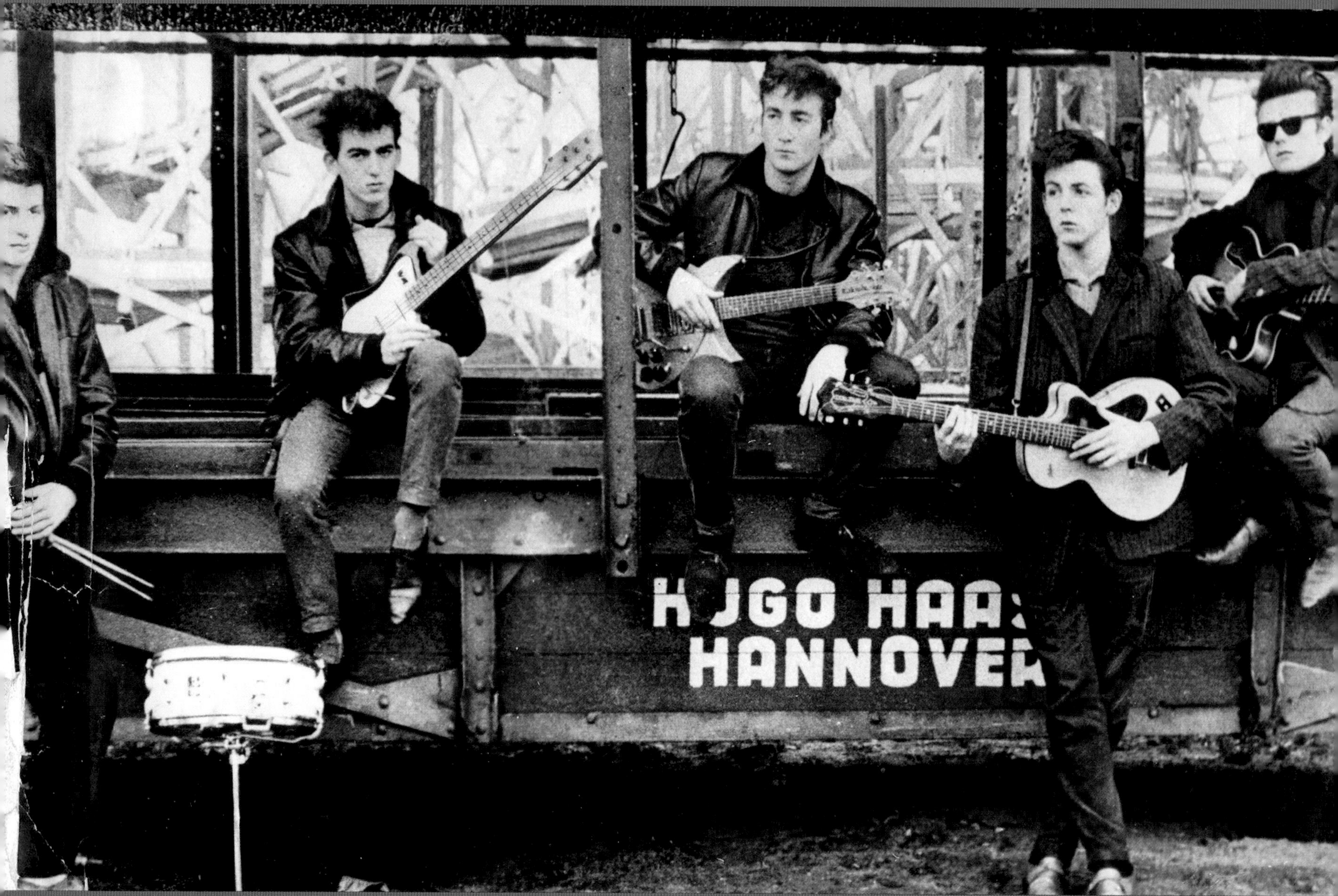
HUGO HAAS
HANNOVER

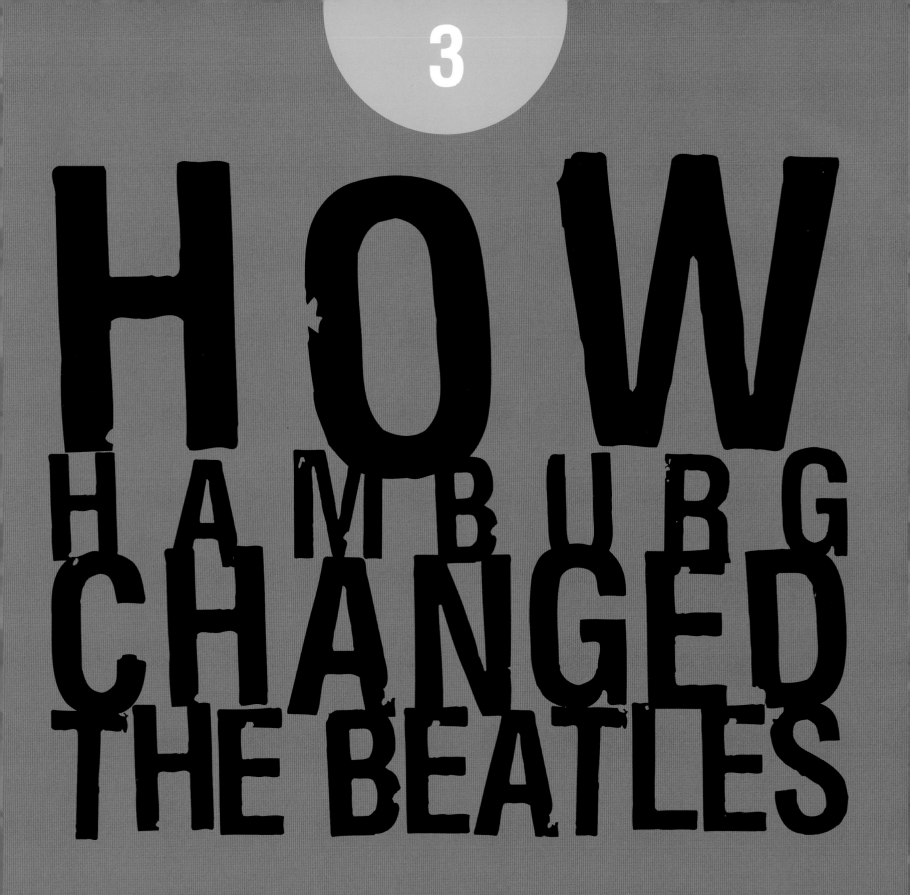

3

HOW
HAMBURG
CHANGED
THE BEATLES

The Quarrymen, 1958
(left to right: George, John, Paul)

It all started when seventeen-year-old John Lennon was a student at Liverpool,

England's, Quarry Bank School, now known as the Calderstones School. Young as he was, he had many passions, and one of them was for a type of music called skiffle. Extremely popular in England, skiffle was based on rock-and-roll and was played with guitars and homemade instruments such as washboards.

In the spring of 1957, after persuading several of his friends to join him, John formed his own skiffle band. At first they called themselves the Blackjacks, but when they discovered that another local group was already using that name, they renamed themselves the Quarrymen, after the name of their school.

Buddy Holly

Like millions of other teenagers on both sides of the Atlantic, John had fallen in love with rock and roll. Among his greatest heroes were American rock stars Elvis Presley, Buddy Holly, Jerry Lee Lewis, and the young musician known as Little Richard. Inspired by both music and the success of the musicians, the Quarrymen's performances were largely made up of songs that these rock and rollers had made popular.

On July 6, 1957, the Quarrymen gave a performance at the St. Peter's Church Garden Fete. In the audience was a fifteen-year-old named Paul McCartney. He had been invited to watch the band perform by one of the members of the group who was impressed with Paul's musical talent. When the event was over, Paul was introduced to John, who quickly discovered that the two of them shared the same musical interests and were in awe of the same rock-and-roll stars. What no one could ever have imagined at the time was that this introduction would lead to one of the greatest songwriting partnerships in musical history. Without hesitation, John invited Paul to join the Quarrymen.

A month after Paul joined the band, another fateful meeting took place. At the end of the group's performance at Liverpool's Wilson Hall, Paul introduced John to a young friend of his whose guitar playing he admired. His name was George Harrison. Paul had urged George not only to attend the performance but also to give John a sample of his playing once it was over. John could not have been more impressed. There was no doubt that George would be a valuable addition to the band. But, as far as John was concerned, there was a big problem. George was only fourteen years old. For his part, George thought playing in a group with John and Paul would be a dream come true. For the better part of the next month, George pleaded his case with John. Finally, convinced that anyone so determined had to be an asset, John took George on. And he not only made him part of the band; he assigned him to play lead guitar.

Given their ages and the stiff competition from many other rock-and-roll groups who made Liverpool their home, it was not easy for the Quarrymen to get bookings. By January 1959, all of John's Quarry Bank School friends had given up and left the group. Even John himself had branched out, taking classes at the Liverpool School of Art. Then, in August, things took a turn. The band, now comprising only John, Paul, and George, was invited to make a series of appearances at a brand-new Liverpool club called the Casbah Coffee Club.

The Casbah was unlike any other Liverpool nightclub or any other nightclub anywhere. It was in the huge basement of a large Victorian house belonging to a woman named Mona Best. One of her sons, Pete, was the eighteen-year-old drummer of a competing band. It was because Pete had been inviting so many of his friends to come to the house to practice their music that Mrs. Best decided to turn her basement into a coffee club for teenagers. Anxious to keep out troublemakers, she organized it as a private club with an annual membership fee of one shilling.

It took six months to convert the space into a suitable place for bands to perform and where some four hundred people could be seated. "Never once during that

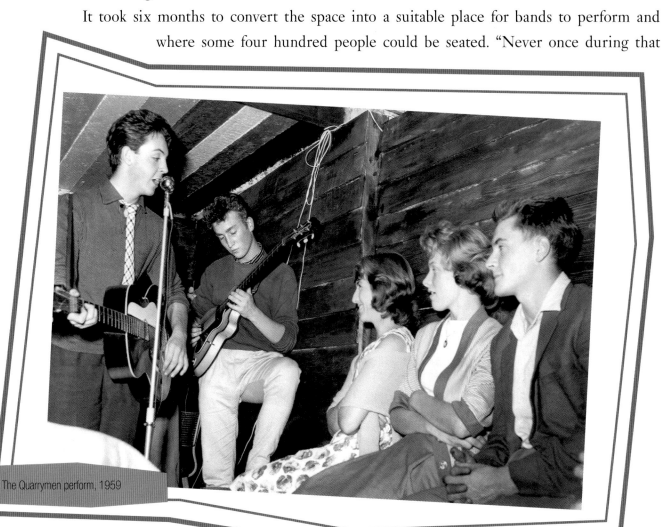

The Quarrymen perform, 1959

exciting six months," Mona Best would later state, "did I ever regret the immense task . . . that I had taken on in deciding to make part of my home a rendezvous for young people. The enthusiasm and the happy atmosphere were wonderful."

Mrs. Best was so persuasive and so determined to make the Casbah a success that by the time it opened on August 29, 1959, more than three hundred teenagers had joined the club. Soon there would be some three thousand members. The Quarrymen—John, Paul, George, and one of John's school friends who played the drums—performed at the Casbah on its opening night. They would go on to make six more appearances at the club.

But it was a temporary respite. Bookings became harder and harder to find, and the group came close to dissolving. Then things took yet another turn. In July 1960, a man named Allan Williams, who had been serving as a part-time manager for the band, arranged for them to appear for at least two months in a nightclub in Hamburg, Germany. What they could not have known was that this would be the turning point in their career. Between mid-August 1960 and the end of December 1962, the band would travel to Hamburg five times. In little more than a year and a half, they would perform for more than 270 nights in a variety of clubs, playing for more than eight hundred hours.

Williams had arranged for the Hamburg booking on one condition. He was not impressed with the various drummers who had played with the band. He insisted they needed to find someone more talented. Paul immediately came up with the answer. Pete Best, whose mother owned the Casbah Club, was a drummer. Both Paul and George had seen Best perform at the club and felt that he would be more than adequate. And Best had something else going for him. At a time when almost no Liverpool musicians could afford to own drums, he owned his own set and could bring it to Hamburg.

Best would not be the only new member of the group. In January 1960, at John's invitation, a handsome young guitar player and artist named Stuart Sutcliffe had joined the band. The group now had a new drummer and a new guitarist. And they were about to get something else. After having undergone a succession of changes in what they had called themselves, they would soon agree on a final name. They would call themselves the Beatles.

On August 16, 1960, John, Paul, George, Pete Best, and Stu Sutcliffe traveled to Hamburg in preparation for their opening at the city's Indra Club two nights later. They were shocked by what they encountered. Before World War II, Hamburg had been Germany's largest seaport and the third-busiest port in the world. But it had been almost completely destroyed in the war. The city that had emerged from the rubble was now known for its many bars, with their raucous and heavy-drinking patrons, and for having more than its share of criminal activity.

As shocked as the band was by the city itself, they were even more taken aback by the living quarters they were given. "We lived backstage . . . [in a movie theater] next to the toilets . . . ," Paul would later describe. "The room had been an old storeroom, and there were just concrete walls and nothing else. No heat, no wallpaper, not a lick of paint; and two sets of bunk beds, like little camp beds, with not very many covers. We were frozen."

On August 18, 1960, the Beatles gave their first performances at the Indra Club. And they were nothing like they had ever done before. The club's owner, Bruno Koschmider, and its rowdy audiences demanded that they play nonstop for almost eight hours at a stretch. And that was not all. Like almost all other bands, the group was used to standing still while it performed. But while the Beatles were playing, Koschmider would continually come to the front of the stage, shouting for them to move around and put on a better show for the customers.

It obviously had its effect. "Once the news got out about that we were making a show, the club started packing them in," Pete Best later recalled. "We played seven nights a week. At first we played almost nonstop till twelve-thirty [at night] when [the club] closed, but as we got better, the crowds stayed till two most mornings." The crowds stayed so late and the music was so loud that a woman who lived in an apartment above the Indra complained to the police, who then ordered Koschmider to halt the rock-and-roll music. Koschmider moved the Beatles and the other acts that were performing at the Indra to another local night-club he owned called the Kaiserkeller.

WHAT'S IN A NAME?

In their earliest days the Beatles had performed under various names, including the Blackjacks, the Quarrymen, Johnny and the Moondogs, and the Moonshiners. One night, when the members of the band arrived for a gig wearing different-colored shirts, it called itself the Rainbows.

For a brief time before beginning their days in Hamburg, the name the Crickets, inspired by one of their heroes, Buddy Holly, had been seriously considered. But, convinced that a cricket was too lowly a creature,

Stu Sutcliff had proposed either Beetles or, maybe better yet, Beatals, denoting a band that beat all competition. A fellow rock and roller, Brian Casser, the lead singer of the group Cass and the Casanovas had his own suggestion. Casser, an obvious admirer of the book *Treasure Island*, told the group that if it was going to name itself after bugs, it should call itself Long John Silver and the Silver Beetles. For a short time the name Silver Beetles was actually adopted.

In the end, it would be John, who had founded the band in the first place, who would give it the name that would stick. As several names were being discussed, John had become convinced that Beatles was the best of them all, not because it denoted beating all competition, but because of the unique musical beat that John felt the group possessed. Later, when he was asked directly why the name Beatles was selected, he responded to his interviewer with characteristic Lennon wit and imagination. "Many people ask what are Beatles?" he stated. "Why Beatles? Ugh, Beatles? How did the name arrive? So we will tell you. It came in a vision—a man appeared on a flaming pie and said unto them, 'From this day on you are Beatles with an "A."' 'Thank you Mister Man,' they said, thanking him. And so they were Beatles."

The Kaiserkeller was larger than the Indra, and it could accommodate even bigger crowds. Inspired by the huge audiences, the band was forced to push itself in whole new ways. "We got better and got more confidence," John would later explain. "We couldn't help it with all the experience playing all night long. It was handy [that the audience spoke a different language]. We had to try even harder, put our heart and soul into it, to get ourselves over. In Liverpool, we'd only ever done one-hour sessions, and we just used to do our best numbers, the same ones, at every one.

In Hamburg, we had to play for eight hours, so we really had to find a new way of playing."

Not surprisingly, the huge crowds that the Beatles were now attracting at the Kaiserkeller did not escape the notice of Hamburg's other nightclub owners. Among them was the owner of the Top Ten Club, who offered the band more money and better living conditions if they would leave the Kaiserkeller and come work for him. Although they were still under contract to Koschmider, the Beatles accepted the offer. But only four of them would make this move. Stu Sutcliffe decided to leave the group to pursue his art studies full-time.

The audiences at the Top Ten were even larger than those at the Kaiserkeller, and the Beatles continually added new songs to their performances to win over new fans. Their marathon performances at the club caught the attention of a fellow Top Ten Club performer, Tony Sheridan. One of Europe's most popular singers, Sheridan asked the group if they would play and sing backup for a recording of the song "My Bonnie" that he was about to make for the German company Polydor Records. The record proved to be a hit, making its way up the German best-seller charts and eventually being released in England. For the Beatles, their first recording was a giant step forward, even though their real band name did not appear on the record. When it came out, it credited the performers as "Tony Sheridan and The Beat Brothers." "They didn't like our name and said, 'Change to the Beat Brothers, this is more understandable for the German audience,'" Paul later explained. "We went along with it . . . it was a record."

There was no question about it. Hamburg was proving to be the best thing that had ever

happened to the Beatles. But then in November 1960, their good fortune ran out. Bruno Koschmider had not taken their abrupt departure from his club lightly. He was furious with them. And he got his revenge. Koschmider knew that, under German law, no one under the age of eighteen was permitted to enter a nightclub, let alone perform in one. But George was only seventeen. That fact had never bothered Koschmider while the Beatles were performing at *his* clubs. But now that they had bolted, he reported George to the German police, who immediately ordered George's deportation back to England. To make matters worse, at about the same time, Paul and Pete were arrested for setting fire to a tapestry that hung on one of the Indra Club's brick walls as a prank. They too were ordered back to England.

After all the success they had enjoyed in Hamburg, the Beatles could not have been more discouraged. What seemed like a bright future was now very much in doubt. But then things changed once again. In February 1961, George turned eighteen. He could now legally perform in German night-clubs. With the aid of some of Pete's mother's influential friends, Paul and Pete got their deportation orders overturned. And the owner of the Top Ten Club made it clear that he wanted the band back as soon as possible.

On April 1, 1961, almost a year after their deportation, the Beatles resumed their performances at the Top Ten Club. When they completed this second stint at the nightclub, which lasted for a full three months, they returned to Liverpool to fulfill a booking that had been arranged for them back at the Cavern Club, where, as the Quarrymen, they had given many of

their earliest performances. The new sound they had developed in Hamburg and their new energetic way of performing both stunned and delighted the club's audiences. This was not the same band that had originally performed at the Cavern. This was something new and exciting. Watching them play, a fellow musician who had seen them perform before they had left for Hamburg commented, "I couldn't believe how good they were [now]. . . . I thought: 'They'll be the first band out of Liverpool to make it.'"

And soon another great change took place. Brian Epstein entered the lives of the Beatles. He was not a musician. He was a businessman. But he had become intrigued with this group called the Beatles when several of the customers at a record store he owned requested the song "My Bonnie" that the group had recorded with Tony Sheridan. On November 9, 1961, Epstein visited the Cavern Club to see for himself what this band was like. It didn't take him long to realize that this group had something special. But they were also undisciplined, he noticed. And their "greasy rocker" image enhanced by their tight, black, all-leather outfits—would never appeal to a wider British public, who expected entertainers to be polished and well dressed.

But Epstein was convinced the band had a lot going for them. They were charming, they were magnetic, and, astoundingly, they had written many of the songs they sang themselves. In Epstein's opinion, the quality of both the melodies and the lyrics of these songs was far superior to that of most rock-and-roll tunes.

Epstein was convinced that this group needed a manager, someone to give them polish. Someone to get them the exposure that would turn them into real stars. Epstein had never managed a band before. He had never even thought of doing so. But for the next three weeks following his Cavern Club visit, he could not drive the thought of managing the Beatles out of his mind. Finally, he acted. On December 3, 1961, he met with the band and offered to manage them. Even he was surprised at how quickly the group, especially John, accepted his offer. "Where's the contract?" John had asked. "I'll sign it."

It did not take Brian Epstein long to put his plans for changing the Beatles into action. Although he met with initial resistance, especially from John, he convinced them that the leather pants and jackets had to go. Within weeks, Epstein's reinvented Beatles were appearing onstage dressed in matching suits with thin lapels and ties.

Then Epstein set out to widen the Beatles' horizons. He began by getting the band an audition at Decca Records. Decca turned them down, but that didn't discourage the determined Epstein. In May 1962, he landed an even bigger prize. George Martin, the extremely talented producer of the Parlophone Company, agreed to sign a contract with the Beatles. For Epstein and the band, it was a huge breakthrough. Parlophone was part of Great Britain's Electric & Musical Industries Ltd (EMI), the largest recording company in the world. It not only arranged recording deals for the entertainers it took on; it booked them in concerts throughout Great Britain and on television shows.

Records, concerts, television appearances—for the Beatles, they were now all exciting prospects. But they also had previous commitments to fulfill. They

Brian Epstein reshaped the Beatles' image.

The Beatles' old look

The Beatles' new look

completed one of them by returning to Hamburg, where, for two months, they appeared at the city's newest nightspot, the Star-Club. Then they returned to England, anxious to begin making records with George Martin.

But as soon as they began their recording sessions, Martin informed Brian Epstein that he had a real problem. While he was convinced that John, Paul, and George were on the way to stardom, he felt just as strongly that Pete Best was holding them back. Pete was pleasant, good-looking, and a fan favorite, but he was not a good enough drummer. Best, Martin declared, had to be replaced.

The task of dismissing Best fell to Epstein. On August 16, 1962, he took the drummer aside and delivered the bad news. Neil Aspinall, who had become the Beatles' road manager, would later recall how Best reacted. "I was in [a] record store looking at records," Aspinall remembered, "and he came down and said he had been fired. He was in a state of shock, really. We went over to the Grapes pub in Matthew Street [and] had a pint."

John would also later give his own account of the firing. "[Pete] was not quick," he would state. "All of us had quick minds, but he never picked that up. The reason he got into the group in the first place was because we had to have a drummer to get to Hamburg.... We were cowards when we sacked him. We made Brian do it. But if we'd told him to his face, that would have been much nastier. It would probably have ended in a fight."

Martin, Epstein, and the rest of the group had not only dismissed Best; they had found his replacement. Wherever they performed in Hamburg, the Beatles had competed for audiences with another band from Liverpool called Rory Storm and the Hurricanes. Its leader, Rory Storm, whose real name was Alan Caldwell, was a true showman. He was an athlete and an acrobat as well. One of the most attention-grabbing antics at any of his band's performances took place when he suddenly shinnied up a pole that ran from the stage to the balcony above. The fact that Storm occasionally fell off the pole only added to the band's allure.

Storm was not the only key member of his band. The group featured a drummer who was as popular with audiences as Storm was. He had been born Richard Starkey, but because he wore so many rings on his fingers and because the name Starr sounded like one of the cowboy movie heroes that he loved to watch, his fellow band members nicknamed him Ringo Starr. The name stuck.

To those who observed both Starr and the Beatles, two things were obvious. Ringo was as funny and quick-witted as Paul, George, and John. He was also a much more versatile and talented drummer than Pete Best. And even though they were competitors in Hamburg, Ringo loved the Beatles. "We would do some gigs at the same venue," Ringo would later explain, "and I started to go and watch them. I just loved the way they played. I loved the songs, the attitude was great, and I knew they

Ringo Starr with Rory Storm and the Hurricanes

were a better band than the one I was in." It was no surprise that when Epstein invited Ringo to replace Pete Best and join the Beatles, he quickly accepted.

On December 17, 1962, the Beatles flew back to Germany for a final two-week stint at the Star-Club. It would be the last time the band ever set foot in Hamburg. But it would be a place they would never forget.

As John would later state, "I might have been born in Liverpool—but I grew up in Hamburg."

Paul would heartily agree, stating that, while the Beatles learned how to play their instruments in Liverpool, it was in Hamburg that they learned how to satisfy an audience.

And they owed even more to what George would call their Hamburg "apprenticeship." As Beatles observer Ian Inglis has written, "The physically grueling and emotionally demanding experience of performing in Hamburg forced the group to become familiar with a wide range of songs and styles; taught them how to perform onstage; and hardened them for competition with their peers. . . ."

Historian Philip Norman perhaps put it best. "They were no good onstage when they went [to Hamburg] and they were very good when they came back," he wrote. "They learned not only stamina. They had to learn an enormous amount of numbers . . . not just rock and roll. . . . They weren't disciplined onstage at all before that. But when they came back, they sounded like no one else. It was the making of them."

As the world would soon discover, it was actually more than the making of them. Thanks to all they had been forced to learn in Hamburg, it was the real beginnings of a band that not only sounded and performed unlike any other, but a group that was about to become first a national and then an international phenomenon.

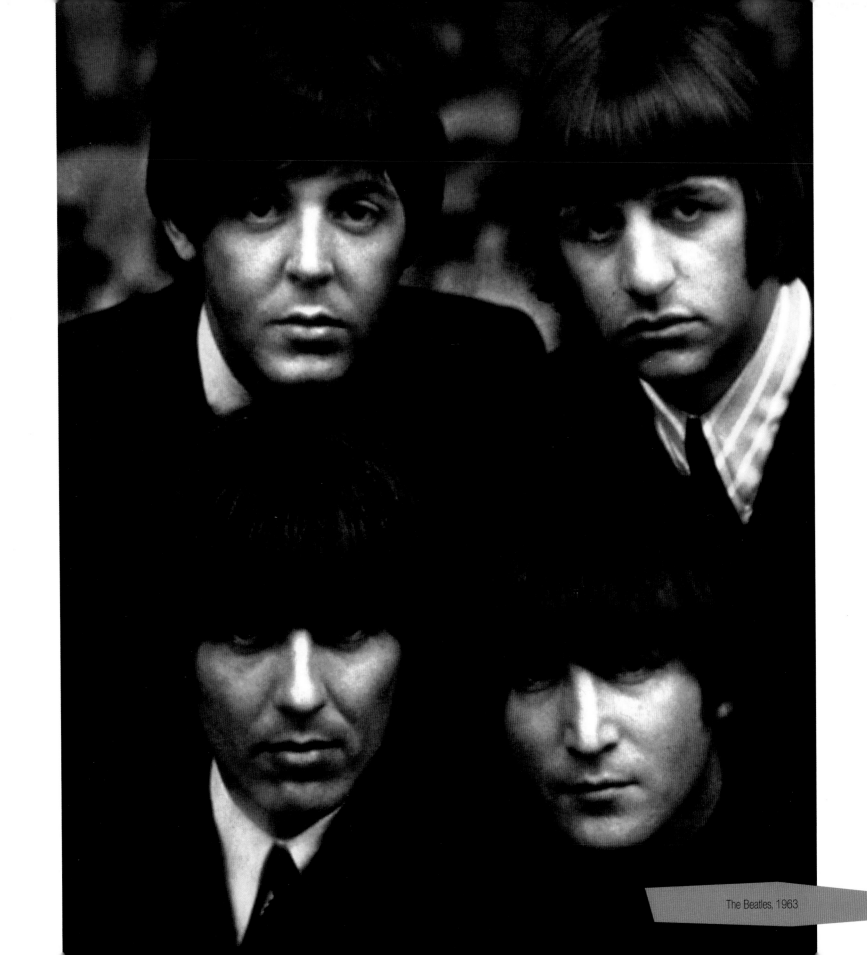

The Beatles, 1963

4

BEATLEMANIA SWEEPS THE WORLD

The soaring success of the Beatles quickly led to a fan frenzy.

For the Beatles, 1963 would be both an exciting and a groundbreaking year. On February 4, their recording of the song "Love Me Do," their first true single, was released in Canada. Almost no one in North America had heard of the band. But as an executive of the company that released the record would say many years later, "I used to listen to about fifty new records a week. Then one day I put on 'Love Me Do' by a group called the Beatles. I immediately sat up and took notice.

The sound was so different, so completely fresh.

I'm certainly not going to claim that I could read the future and already knew how big the Beatles were going to be, but I did like them a lot and I wanted [my company] to get in on the ground floor."

Later in February, Parlphone released the Beatles' second single, "Please Please Me." It became the group's first number-one single in Great Britain. This breakthrough hit was quickly followed by the Beatles' first album, also called *Please Please Me*, and by their third single, "From Me to You," which also climbed to the top of the British bestselling charts.

The Beatles then embarked on several brief concert tours. Brief as they were, the tours led to something that had never before been seen in Great Britain. Everywhere the Beatles went, near riots broke out. John, Paul, George, and Ringo were mobbed when they attempted to leave their hotel or when they left their car and attempted to enter the avenue where they were about to play.

By this time, the BBC had adopted the Beatles as its own. After the Beatles made many radio appearances, the BBC gave them a radio series, titled *Pop Go the Beatles*. The band began to perform so many times on BBC Television that some of the media began referring to it as the "Beatles Broadcasting Corporation." A monthly magazine titled *The Beatles Book* had also made its appearance. The official Beatles Fan Club, which had begun with a few thousand teenagers, now boasted a membership of more than seventy thousand.

George and Ringo disguised as police

In the fall of 1963, the Beatles' record "She Loves You" was released. It quickly became their biggest hit yet. And it set the stage for an extraordinary happening. On October 13, the band appeared on a live television program, *Saturday Night at the London Palladium*. Even hours before the program went on the air, thousands of young Beatles fans began arriving at the Palladium. London police could hardly control them. The stage door to the enormous

Beatles at the Palladium

theater was blocked by huge piles of presents and letters put there by the adoring fans. When the Beatles attempted to rehearse their numbers, they could hardly be heard over the chanting and screaming teenagers outside.

Amazing as the scene around the Palladium was, even more astounding was what took place in homes throughout Great Britain that night. More than fifteen million people sat in front of their televisions watching the Beatles. As author Hunter Davies has written, "[It was on] the night of October 13, 1963, that the Beatles stopped being simply an interesting pop-music story and became front-page hard news in every national newspaper." The lads from Liverpool had become a national phenomenon.

Three weeks later, the phenomenon grew ever bigger. As popular as *Saturday Night at the Palladium* was, the biggest and by far most glamorous British entertainment event of every year was the variety show known both as the *Royal Command Performance* and the *Royal Variety Performance.* Those chosen to appear on the show were selected by the British royal family, who made every effort to attend. Told that the family had not only asked that the Beatles be included, but that they headline the show, Brian Epstein would exclaim that it "was an even greater honor than the Palladium."

The 1963 event was a particularly glittering affair attended by many members of the royal family, including the Queen Mother and Queen Elizabeth's sister Princess Margaret. The Queen herself would have attended but she was pregnant and not feeling well. Also among the audience were scores of members of England's highest society. They were joined by hundreds of other adults hoping to get a close look at the royal family. In sharp contrast to them all were the thousands of young Beatles fans, straining against the police barricades, chanting,

"We want the Beatles, we want the Beatles."

The audience that night was treated not only to a spirited Beatles performance of four of their songs, but to a display of their now-famous wit. Introducing a tune, John looked out at the audience and asked the people in the cheaper seats to clap their hands in time to the song. Then, turning to the royal box, he shouted, "Those upstairs, just rattle your jewelry." It was the first time that any entertainer had ever publicly poked fun at the royal family. Brian Epstein, in particular, immediately was concerned about what the reaction would be to John's good-natured remark. But the next day, England's newspapers were unanimous in commenting that it was a remark that only a group as beloved as the Beatles could get away with.

When the show was over, Princess Margaret, who had been seen happily snapping her fingers during the Beatles' numbers, made a point of shaking hands with John, Paul, George, and Ringo. She had had real trouble reaching them because as soon as the final curtain had come down, the band had been mobbed by their young fans. So many of them insisted on remaining in the theater that the police were forced to lock the Beatles in their dressing room for thirteen hours before they finally felt it was safe for them to leave.

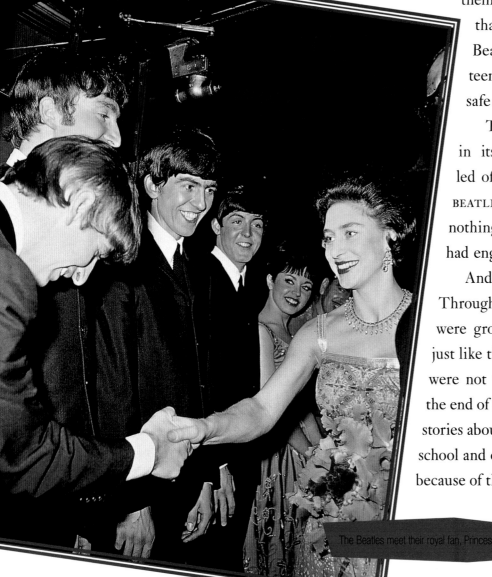

The Beatles meet their royal fan, Princess Margaret.

The next day London's *Daily Mirror*, in its front-page account of the show, led off its story with the banner headline BEATLEMANIA. It was only one word. But nothing could have better described what had engulfed all of England.

And it could be seen everywhere. Throughout Great Britain, teenage boys were growing their hair long and styling it just like that of their heroes. Horrified parents were not the only ones who disapproved. By the end of the year, newspapers were filled with stories about boys who had been sent home from school and of young apprentices being dismissed because of their Beatle hairdos.

The madness surrounding the Beatles grew even stronger. In November, at a show in Plymouth, England, hoses had to be turned on a crowd of young Beatle fans to keep them under control. In Portsmouth, a riot took place when the Beatles' performance was canceled because Paul had come down with the flu. Newspapers in the area issued hourly reports on his condition. He quickly recovered, but in Birmingham, the only way the Beatles were able to escape from a hysterical crowd was to disguise themselves as policemen.

It was not only the Beatles whose safety was in jeopardy. The fans endangered themselves with their frenzied behavior. In the tiny town of Carlisle, more than six hundred teenagers, determined to get tickets for an upcoming Beatles show, stood in line for thirty-six hours in freezing weather, waiting for the box office to open. When it finally did, the crowd rushed forward with such force that nine young people were trampled and taken to the hospital. Police reported that at least a dozen girls in the crowd had fainted.

Through it all, sales of Beatles records and albums continued to reach amazing new heights. Advance orders for the band's new album, *With the Beatles,* soared to 250,000. By the end of the year, the Beatles, whom the press was now calling the Fab Four, had Britain's bestselling album *Please Please Me;* the top-selling extended-play record, "Twist and Shout"; and the top-selling single, "She Loves You."

It was not only music that came to symbolize Beatlemania. Everywhere throughout Great Britain, people were anxious to get their hands on anything that had to do with the group. Officials at the schools in Liverpool that the Beatles had attended were swamped with requests for anything the boys had touched—pens, pencils, erasers, school caps. Letters came in offering to pay a princely sum for any desk that had once been sat at by a future Beatle. Soon, enterprising individuals were selling composition books supposedly signed by a young John or Paul or George or Ringo. The fact that none of them were authentic did nothing to hinder their sales.

For the Beatles, 1963 had been an unbelievable year. They had conquered Great Britain. But it was only the beginning. During the final week of October 1963, the Fab Four played a series of concerts in Sweden. On October 31, they flew back to England. By this time they had gotten used to mob scenes wherever they appeared. In Sweden, the presence of scores of police with guard dogs had barely kept the crowds under control. During one of the concerts, fans had actually broken through a police barrier and managed to get onto the stage. The police

Letter to Ringo

had been able to restore order, but not before George had been knocked down by an adoring crowd.

Nothing, however, had prepared them for what they encountered when they landed back in England. Thousands of young fans had been pouring into London's Heathrow Airport for hours before the group's scheduled arrival. The roads leading to the airport had become so clogged with teenagers that the car carrying England's prime minister, who was on his way to an overseas meeting, could not get through. Inside the airport, some of the most beautiful young women in the world, arriving in London to compete in the Miss World contest, were almost totally ignored by the growing crowd intent only on seeing the Beatles.

For the Beatles themselves, their triumphant return to England was a revelation. They would later state that it was the overwhelming greeting they received at the airport that first made them aware of just how popular they had become. For them, as they would also later proclaim, the Beatlemania craze really began on that Halloween at Heathrow.

The prime minister and the Miss World contestants were not the only celebrities at Heathrow that day. Also present was one of the most recognizable men in America. His name was Ed Sullivan, and he was the host of *The Ed Sullivan Show*, a television variety program watched by millions of Americans every Sunday night. Ed Sullivan was much more than a television host. He was a star maker. So many people regularly watched his live show that, for almost any entertainer, an appearance on the program was a career highlight. For new talent, performing on *The Ed Sullivan Show* was often the ticket to becoming a household name.

Sullivan had landed at Heathrow after completing a talent-search tour of Europe, and he was astounded to see thousands of young people jamming the airport. Even though it was raining heavily, a huge throng of screaming teenagers was perched on the terminal's flat roof. Asking someone what the commotion was all about, Sullivan was told it was for the Beatles, who were returning from Sweden. When he asked who in the world the Beatles were, he was told simply that they were a popular British band.

When he returned to America, Sullivan, intrigued by the pandemonium he had witnessed

at the London airport, had his aides contact Brian Epstein to ask about the possibility of the Beatles appearing on his show. Epstein recognized this as the band's chance to make it big in America. Epstein immediately flew to New York, where, thanks to Beatlemania, he made a deal for the Beatles to appear on *The Ed Sullivan Show*, setting the stage for the night that changed America.

At that time, the Beatles were still largely unknown in America. But not completely. On December 10, America's leading news anchor, Walter Cronkite, had included a brief clip of the Beatles performing their song "She Loves You" on his news program. Among the viewers who had seen the program was fifteen-year-old Marsha Albert of Silver Springs, Maryland. Immediately after watching it, she wrote a letter to her favorite radio station, WWDC, asking why people in the United States had not been able to listen to the Beatles' music. The radio station's disc jockey, Carroll James, who had also seen the brief clip, then made arrangements to have the Beatles' latest record, a song called "I Want to Hold Your Hand," shipped immediately to him from England by airplane.

On December 17, 1963, exactly a week after the Cronkite broadcast, James invited Marsha Albert to come down to the radio station to introduce "I Want to Hold Your Hand" on his show. When the show ended, James asked his listeners to write to him, giving their opinion of the Beatles. The response was beyond anything that the disc jockey could have imagined. Instead of writing to James, hundreds of callers began phoning the station, praising both the song and the Beatles themselves. So many calls came in that the station's switchboard could not handle the volume.

Astounded by this reaction, James made a copy of the recording and sent it to a disc jockey in Chicago. When that man played it on his station, he too became swamped with praise for

BEATLES BOOSTERS

At the time that the Beatles were preparing to come to the United States, radio was still extremely popular and a number of radio disc jockeys, like Carroll James, were as well-known to their listeners as the performers whose songs they played. The Beatles were so grateful to James for having initiated the enormous sales of "I Want to Hold Your Hand" that, when they played their first American concert at the Washington Coliseum, they arranged for him to be the master of ceremonies of the event.

James, however, was far from the only disc jockey, or deejay, as they were also called, to bolster the Fab Four's American success. Dick Biondi, who, at one time or another in the 1950s and 1960s, was a disc jockey at leading radio stations in Buffalo, Chicago, and Los Angeles, was also a huge Beatles booster. His great claim to fame was that even before James played "I Want to Hold Your Hand" on Washington's radio station WWDC, Biondi had played the band's "Please Please Me" on Chicago's radio station WLS.

Among the most influential of all the Beatles-boosting disc jockeys was Bruce Morrow, known to his loyal listeners at New York's radio station WABC as "Cousin Brucie." Along with continually playing Beatles songs, Morrow was able to periodically arrange exclusive interviews with the Fab Four. And on one occasion he was able to gain a huge publicity bonanza for his station. While conducting an interview with the Beatles, Morrow learned that Ringo, while entering a New York hotel, had had his St. Christopher's medal snatched from around his neck by an overzealous young fan. While his tens of thousands of listeners were tuned in, he launched a daily appeal for the return of the medal. Morrow's appeals became a media sensation that ultimately convinced the remorseful fan to give back the stolen medal.

Fans listened to Beatles hits on transistor radios.

Despite all this, however, Morrow was not the most influential Beatles-boosting disc jockey. That honor went to radio station WINS disc jockey Murray Kaufman, known to listeners as Murray the K. He reached the height of his popularity in the mid-1960s, when he not only made the playing of the Fab Four's songs on his program his number-one priority but also became a Beatles insider by traveling with them on each of their North American tours. It was an association that led the never-modest Kaufman to proclaim himself to be nothing less than the "Fifth Beatle."

Murray the K

Although radio disc jockeys no longer enjoy the prominence they once had in the broadcasting world, there are still radio deejays and they still play the Beatles' music. Most notable of them all is Las Vegas disc jockey Dennis Mitchell, whose radio program "Dennis Mitchell's Breakfast with the Beatles" has been running continually for nearly twenty years. "A lot of my audience is about my age [53] . . . ," Mitchell says, "but the most enthusiastic messages I get are from people who are in their 20s, [who describe the Beatles' music and their story as] unbelievable."

the song and the Beatles. Somehow, a station in St. Louis also obtained a tape of the recording. After their disc jockey aired it, that station also became deluged with requests to play the song as many times each day as possible.

The stations in Washington, DC; Chicago; and St. Louis were thrilled that so many listeners were tuning in to hear a recording still available for sale only in England. But not everyone was so pleased. Capitol Records, the company for whom the Beatles had recorded the song, had planned to begin selling it in America on January 13, 1964. But with stations in three of the largest cities in the United States playing it over and over again, Capitol immediately began sending the record to stores throughout America. They realized that radio airplay was key to the recording's sales success.

The result was phenomenal. In the first three days of its release in the United States, more than 250,000 copies of "I Want to Hold Your Hand" were sold. By the middle of January, some ten thousand copies of the record sold each hour in New York City alone, and the total number of sales in the United States had reached over one million. Thanks initially to young Marsha Albert, the Beatles came to America riding a huge wave of success.

As the day of the Beatles' American trip fast approached, the nation's leading magazines and newspapers took up the cry. "First England fell, victim of a million girlish

The iconic Capitol Records Tower, which is widely believed to look like a stack of records on a turntable

screams," *Life* magazine proclaimed. "Then Paris surrendered. Now the United States must brace itself."

Some of the news journals had gone beyond informing their readers that the Beatles were on their way, and had issued a warning as well. "'The Beatles are coming,'" wrote the *Baltimore Evening Sun*. "Those four words are said to be enough to jelly the spine of the most courageous police captains in Britain. . . . Since, in this case, the Beatles are coming to America, America had better take thought as to how it will deal with the invasion." It could not have been a more prophetic warning.

5

HOW THE BEATLES CHANGED THE MOVIES

Elvis movie poster

Given their phenomenal popularity and the fact

they were so clever, funny, and photogenic, it was not surprising that the Beatles would be called upon to make movies. And in doing so, they would change the world of motion pictures almost as dramatically as they had changed the world of popular music.

The Beatles were not the first rock-and-roll stars to make movies. It was, in fact, expected that these performers would capitalize on their fame by trying their hand at acting and seeking the further glamour and money that came with starring in a motion picture. Elvis Presley had made many movies. So had Chuck Berry, Bill Haley, and Little Richard. The films they made were mostly undistinguished. Many of them were panned by critics and brought nothing new either to movies themselves or to the art of moviemaking.

The Beatles, on the other hand, and Richard Lester, the man who directed their films, were determined to make their movies as revolutionary as their music. And in their first two films in particular they did just that, bringing innovations that continue to influence the way movies and television shows are made today.

The first of these movies was titled *A Hard Day's Night*. Released in 1964, the film had a simple plot involving John, Paul, George, and Ringo engaged in an ongoing series of madcap escapades. The film was designed to give moviegoers an inside look at Beatlemania. But it turned out to be much more.

When the Beatles began their moviemaking, all motion pictures were tightly scripted and the actors and actresses religiously recited the lines in the script. Movies were typically made up of long scenes in which the performers' movements were also tightly scripted. The dialogue in *A Hard Day's Night* was short and punchy, and it was often made up on the spot by the Fab Four. The loosely scripted scenes were also short and rapid-fire. Most important, each of the scenes was edited to the beat of accompanying Beatles songs, bringing music and images together in a way that had never been seen in the movies, making *A Hard Day's Night* the fastest-paced motion picture that had ever been made.

Equally revolutionary were the technical innovations that Lester brought to the film. The contrasting long shots and close-ups, and the unique camera angles, the use of a hand-held camera were startling cinematic advancements that would soon be copied by countless moviemakers.

Most important of all, *A Hard Day's Night* would provide the Beatles with an opportunity to share the types of messages that would increasingly be embodied in their songs in a new, visual medium. The movie was a brilliantly done comedy. It brought enormous attention to how exciting rock music could be. But it was also about youth and its desire to escape from injustices, a theme that continues to make *A Hard Day's Night* as relevant today as when it was made.

The movie company that funded *A Hard Day's Night* did so because it was anxious to secure the rights to the movie's sound track, knowing that, because of the Beatles, it could be turned into a bestselling album. It had no idea that it was funding a movie that would gain such

extraordinary acclaim. Even those critics who had not been caught up in Beatlemania heralded the excitement the Beatles had brought to the screen. "Though I don't pretend to understand what makes these four rather odd-looking boys so fascinating to so many scores of millions of people," one highly respected movie critic wrote, "I admit that I feel a certain mindless joy stealing over me as they caper about uttering sounds."

Even more important was the fact that so many of the critics recognized how the Beatles had changed the world of movies. It is a recognition that continues today. As Roger Ebert, legendary movie critic once wrote, "When we watch TV and see quick cutting, hand-held cameras, interviews conducted on the run with moving targets, quickly intercut snatches of dialogue, music under documentary action and all the other trademarks of the modern style, we are looking at the children of *A Hard Day's Night*."

In their film debut, the Beatles had proven themselves to be as witty, charming, and captivating as they were on the stage. And they had made the movie under the same unique circumstances that had come to characterize most of their live performances. Remembering the days spent making *A Hard Day's Night*, Richard Lester recalled how making the film as innovative as possible was not the only challenge.

Michael Bay filming *Transformers*

RINGO'S TONSILS

The way in which the Beatles had to continually flee from their adoring fans while making their movies was one example of the unprecedented attention everything about them inspired. Even Ringo's tonsils caused an uproar.

During one of the Fab Four's worldwide tours, Ringo was stricken with tonsillitis and had to have his tonsils removed. Thanks to a gigantic mistake made by a BBC announcer, it sent thousands of Beatles fans into shock.

Like everything else relating to the Beatles, the removal of Ringo's tonsils was big news. But when the BBC was given the news of the surgery's completion, its announcer Roy Williams misread the news bulletin. Millions of BBC listeners were tuned in when Williams announced, "Ringo Starr's TOENAILS were successfully removed this morning." Immediately, the network's switchboard was jammed with calls from agonized fans. Williams later apologized for his blunder, stating, "I misread the item. It happens to all of us and I bet Ringo is glad I'm not his surgeon."

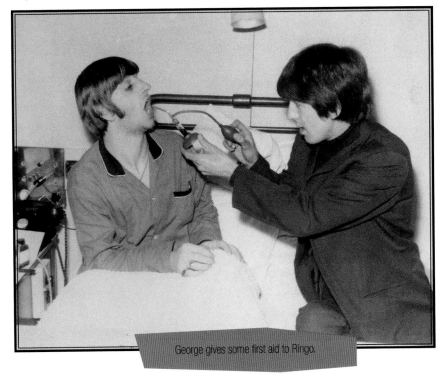

George gives some first aid to Ringo.

Ringo's neighbors actually benefited from his infirmity. "Ringo's tonsil operation has given us our first peace in months," exclaimed a man who lived close to the Beatles' drummer. "Teenage girls scream and shriek all day long. They get hysterical, fight and kick each other and chase every car that arrives in case Ringo is inside." Told of his neighbor's comments, a sympathetic Ringo replied, "I wish I could do something about it—but I can't control the fans."

Beatles running from fans during filming of *A Hard Day's Night*

"Wherever we set up," he stated, **"the word would instantly get out that the Beatles were there. After about three takes, we'd all have to run for our lives."**

The Fab Four's second movie, the 1965 film titled *Help!* was a much more lavish production than *A Hard Day's Night*. Filmed in full color and shot on locations around the world, it was a spoof of the James Bond movies and other adventure films that had become so popular. Like *A Hard Day's Night*, it would be characterized by an ongoing series of fast-paced scenes that would directly influence how future highly successful television series such as *Monty Python's Flying Circus* and *The Monkees* would be made. As one modern-day critic has stated, "Every sketch comedy show on cable or broadcast owes something to *Help!*"

In addition to *A Hard Day's Night* and *Help!* the Beatles would make three other feature films: *Magical Mystery Tour* (1967), *Yellow Submarine* (1968), and *Let It Be* (1970). Most notable of these would be *Yellow Submarine*, a 1968 animated musical fantasy based on the Fab Four's music. Except for a brief clip at the end of the film, the Beatles did not appear in the movie. Instead, their voices were impersonated by actors. Along with such established Beatles hits as "Yellow Submarine," "All You Need Is Love," "Eleanor Rigby," "Nowhere Man," and "When I'm

Sixty-Four," the film introduced five new Beatles songs, including the inspirational "All Together Now," which would eventually be recorded by various artists in several different countries.

Just as *A Hard Day's Night* and *Help!* would change the world of movies, *Yellow Submarine* proved to be groundbreaking as well. Not only would the film be hailed by audiences and critics alike, but it would become widely credited with establishing animation as a serious art form.

All the Fab Four's enduring innovations in moviemaking would lead to something else we owe to the Beatles. Today, music companies frequently promote their offerings through music videos. They have become a staple of the entertainment industry, embraced by young people and adults throughout the world.

The music video was invented by the Beatles in 1966. Before then, the only way that performers could promote their latest records was through live appearances on radio or television. But by 1966 the Beatles were far too busy to meet the overwhelming demand for promotional appearances. Inspired by the acclaim that several segments of both *A Hard Day's Night* and *Help!* continued to receive, they decided to create a video containing their new songs "Rain" and "Paperback Writer" and send copies to broadcast outlets on both sides of the Atlantic.

Buoyed by the success of this revolutionary promotion, in 1967 the Beatles created two other musical videos, one for their song "Strawberry Fields Forever," and the other for "Penny Lane." Even more sophisticated than the first video, these, in the tradition of the Beatles' first two movies, were marked by fast-paced images of the Fab Four cut to the beat of their music,

Liverpool's Penny Lane inspired the hit song and a groundbreaking music video.

dramatic lighting, unprecedented camera techniques, and one of the first uses of slow motion.

It was the beginning of what has become one of the world's most popular forms of entertainment. Given the enormous technological advances that have been made in the last fifty years, today's music videos are far more sophisticated than even the Beatles could have imagined. With their fully developed story lines, many of them are actually mini-movies. But it all started with the Beatles. It was an accomplishment that George, in particular, would acknowledge. Late in his career, when asked to comment on the influence the Beatles' music videos had, he answered simply. "I suppose," he stated, "in a way, we invented MTV."

The MTV Video Music Award celebrates the art of music videos by awarding the Moonman statue.

The Beatles made promotional films for "Paperback Writer" and "Rain," which were among the first music videos ever produced.

PLACES MADE FAMOUS BY THE BEATLES

The promotional videos the Beatles created for their songs "Strawberry Fields Forever" and "Penny Lane" set the stage for all musical videos to follow. Both of these songs, which became enormous hits, were based on actual places.

Although it is usually credited to both John and Paul, "Strawberry Fields Forever" was actually written by John alone and was inspired by his memories of having played in the garden of a Liverpool orphanage named Strawberry Field as a child. While the song was named for the original Strawberry Field, it is another Strawberry Fields that has become even more famous.

In 1981, wishing to pay tribute to John's contributions as a songwriter, musician, and peace activist, the New York City Council designated a 2.5-acre area of the city's Central Park as "Strawberry Fields." In the center of the area lies a large, circular mosaic bearing the word "Imagine," the title of one of John's most inspiring songs. Created by Italian craftsmen and donated by the city of Naples, the mosaic "evokes a vision and hope for a world without strife, war and conflict," in the words of the Central Park Conservancy. Nearby the mosaic is a bronze plaque that lists the names of more than 120 countries that have planted flowers and donated money for the maintenance of the area. Since its erection, visitors from all over the world continue to flock to the site, particularly on the anniversaries of John's birth and death.

Strawberry Field orphanage

When the song "Strawberry Fields Forever" was released, the other side of the record contained the song "Penny Lane." The Beatles' producer George Martin regarded it as probably the greatest single ever created. Like "Strawberry Fields Forever," "Penny

"Imagine" tribute in New York's Central Park

Lane" expresses nostalgia for past places and past times. And like Strawberry Field, it is a real place—the name of a Liverpool street near John's childhood home.

From the time it was released, the popularity of the song "Penny Lane" created a real problem for Liverpool officials. Beatles fans kept stealing the street signs bearing its name. To combat this, the officials stopped replacing the signs and painted the name on the side of buildings. In 2007, however, thanks to modern technology, theft-proof signs were specially created, and Penny Lane street signs reappeared.

The most visited of all the places made famous by their association with the Beatles is the London thoroughfare known as Abbey Road. Actually, it is not the road itself but a crosswalk leading to Abbey Road studios, where the Fab Four recorded their most creative albums, that has become a mecca for Beatles fans. The photograph of the Fab Four walking in step from left to right across the road to the studio, which became the cover of the band's *Abbey Road* album, is one of music's most famous and enduring images.

In the spring of 2012, interest in the photograph that has been described as depicting "one of the most historic moments in not just the Beatles' history, but also rock-and-roll history" accelerated when twenty-five previously unknown pictures, taken on the same day, were discovered. The photographs show the Fab Four in the same crosswalk, but moving in the opposite direction. In May 2012, just one of these images sold at auction for more than $25,000.

The famous crosswalk by Abbey Road studio

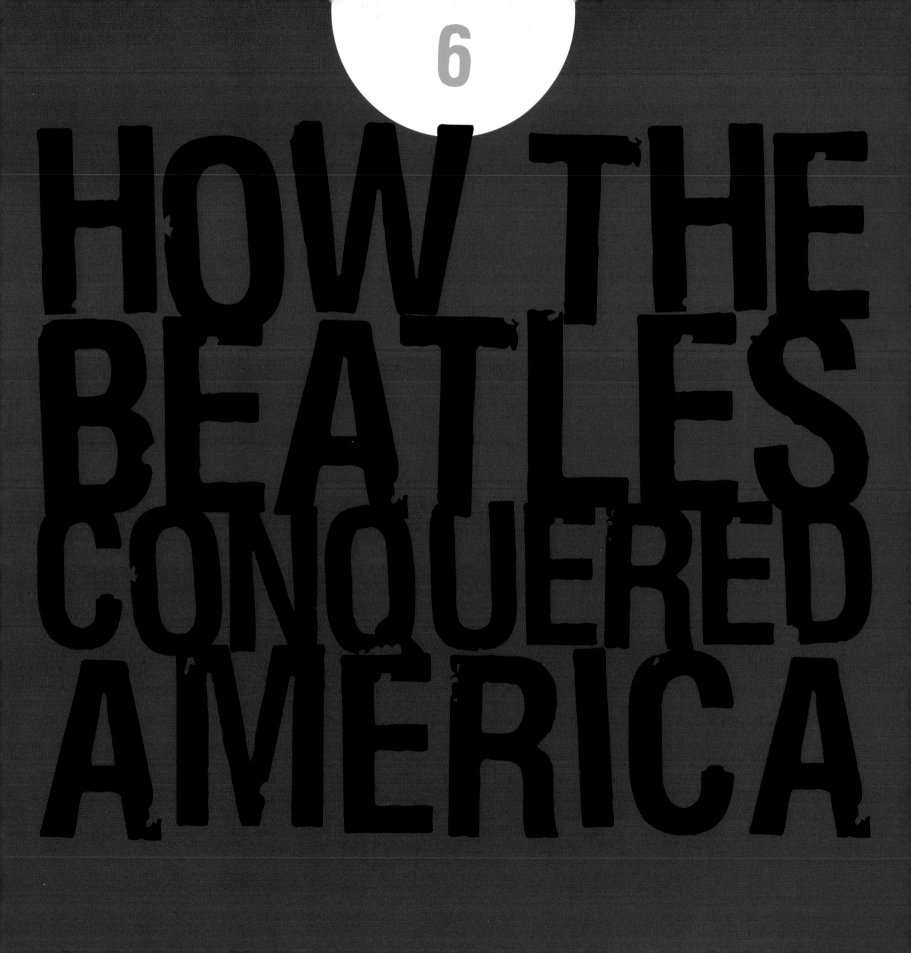

6

HOW THE BEATLES CONQUERED AMERICA

WWDC
WELCOMES
THE BEATLES

The Beatles arriving at Union Station in Washington

As the Beatles had prepared to cross the Atlantic to appear on *The Ed Sullivan Show*, newspapers and magazines had warned Americans to brace themselves for nothing short of an invasion. What they didn't predict was that the *Sullivan Show* appearance would be just the beginning of that invasion.

The Beatles had had little time to celebrate the triumph they achieved with their first live American television appearance. They had been booked to give their first live American concert just two days later in Washington, DC's, Washington Coliseum.

The plan had been for the Beatles and their ever-growing entourage of reporters and photographers to fly from New York to Washington, DC. But when they awoke on February 11, they were greeted by a raging snowstorm. George, in particular, made it known that there was no way he was going to fly in that weather. The others readily agreed. They would take the train. Quickly, a private railroad car was found and attached to the New York to Washington train. It was no ordinary car. Taken out of retirement for this one trip, it was an elegant early-English railroad coach.

The arrival at Washington's Union Station was as wild as the band's landing in New York had been. More than three thousand screaming teenagers were waiting to greet them. Many were flinging themselves against the twenty-foot-high iron platform gates, trying to get at the Beatles as they stepped off the train.

The concert that night was every bit as chaotic. More than twenty thousand fans packed the Coliseum. And hundreds of them had brought something with them. Before the Beatles had left England, a British journalist had reported that the boys loved the British version of jelly beans, called jelly babies. As soon as the Beatles began playing, the young fans began affectionately throwing jelly beans at them. Some even tossed full, unopened bags of the mini-missiles at their heroes. "It was terrible," George stated. "They hurt. They don't have soft jelly babies in America but hard jelly beans like bullets."

A Beatles snowball fight

Aside from the jelly bean barrage, the Washington concert was marked by something that would become characteristic of many Beatles concerts that followed. From the moment of the first chord, the audience's hysterical screaming was so loud that the Beatles could barely hear their instruments, let alone their singing. The ecstatic teenagers didn't mind a bit. They were there to see the Beatles, not necessarily to hear them. Most important, they would be able to brag to their friends that they had seen them *in person.*

For the Beatles themselves, their first concert in the United States, coming on the heels of their phenomenal first American television success, was nothing short of a triumph. Paul thought that the concert was even more exciting than the television appearance had been. Ringo was the most vocal of all. "What an audience!" he exclaimed. "I could have played all night."

But once again there would be little time to celebrate or even reflect upon their latest triumph. The day after the Washington concert, the Beatles were on the move again, this time back to New York. They had been booked to appear in Carnegie Hall, the most prestigious and famous concert hall in America. The goal of every classical musical artist had long been to appear at Carnegie Hall. The world's greatest opera singers, violinists, pianists, and symphony orchestras had graced its stage. Never had a rock group played there. Never had it even been imagined that such a thing could happen.

On the morning of February 12, even as the Beatles' train pulled out of Washington, thousands of young people headed for New York's Pennsylvania Station to meet the train. It was Lincoln's Birthday, schools were

Carnegie Hall poster announcing Beatles concert

not in session, and the crowd standing by the track where the train was to arrive grew larger by the minute. When railroad police saw what was happening, they called ahead to the train and had it rerouted to a different, more remote track. As the Beatles stepped off the train, they were hustled into a freight elevator. Once they reached the street above, they were smuggled into an unmarked car and whisked away to the Plaza Hotel.

The Plaza was surrounded by hysterical young fans, but after a quick shower and change of clothes, John, Paul, George, and Ringo were hustled off into a back elevator and led out of the hotel through its kitchen. They were then driven to Carnegie Hall in a taxicab rather than the limousine that the crowd camped out at the hotel was expecting them to take.

The schedule called for the band to give two concerts that evening, one at 7:45 and the other at 11:15. Both performances completely sold out less than a day after they had gone on sale, and when the band arrived backstage, they were greeted by a mob scene. By now they were used to chaotic adulation. But this was different. Those who had been allowed backstage were not the Beatles' usual young admirers. They included well-known celebrities—movie stars, sports heroes, political figures, and the wife of New York's governor. Some of the most famous people in America had climbed aboard the Beatles bandwagon. And they were acting no differently from the band's teenage fans—crowding up as close to them as they could, barraging them with questions, pleading for autographs.

In order to accommodate as many of those frantic to see the Beatles as possible, the concert's promoters had set up scores of chairs on the stage itself, leaving the band just a small space on which to perform. John, the most outspoken and sometimes most cantankerous of the group, was not reluctant to express his opinion of it all. "They had all these people sitting on the stage with us," he later exclaimed. "It wasn't a rock show; it was just a sort of circus where we were in cages. We were being pawed and talked at and met and touched, backstage and onstage. We were just like animals."

Despite the mayhem, the band's two performances were enormously successful. Both audiences went wild. As the Associated Press reported the next day, the Beatles "tore the roof off Carnegie Hall" and "set off a crescendo of teen-age squeals that could almost be heard across the river to New Jersey." Something else had taken place as well. Thanks to the Beatles, other popular music groups would soon be invited to perform at venerable Carnegie Hall.

Amazingly, the Beatles' frantic pace continued. Their second live *Ed Sullivan Show* appearance was planned for Miami on February 16, just four days after the Carnegie Hall concerts.

The Beatles had been shocked by the greeting they received when their plane touched down in New York. They had been amazed at the public reaction only two days later at the train station in Washington. But nothing could have prepared them for their arrival at the Miami airport.

Seven thousand teens had gathered inside the airport building. As soon as the Beatles' plane landed, the fans rushed forward. In their frenzy to get out of the building and as close to their idols as they could, they broke through twenty-three glass windows and doors. It was, as a Miami newspaper reported, "a smashing welcome . . . smashed doors, smashed windows, smashed furniture, a smashed auto roof."

The Beatles, the newspaper stated, "were nearly squashed when . . . scores of screaming teens broke through police lines and hurled themselves at limousines waiting to whisk the Beatles away."

The scene at the Deauville Hotel, where the Beatles would be staying and from which *The Ed Sullivan Show* would be televised, was just as frantic. While a large police escort whisked the boys up to their rooms, hordes of young fans surrounded the hotel, hoping to get a glimpse of their heroes. And some of them were

Fun in the sun in Miami

intent on getting more than a glimpse. In the most imaginative attempt of all, two girls had themselves wrapped in two huge packages addressed to the Beatles. Unfortunately for them, their bold plan was discovered before they could be personally delivered to Paul or John or George or Ringo.

The Ed Sullivan Show was still a few days away. The band had time to relax and have some fun, an exceedingly rare occurence. Members of the hotel staff taught them to snorkel in one of the Deauville's enormous pools. Accompanied by legions of reporters and police escorts, they went on shopping sprees where they happily purchased large amounts of American-style clothing. They got to go to what they regarded as an American phenomenon—a drive-in movie. A

Miami car dealer, as awestruck by the young celebrities as were their teenage fans, lent each of them a sports car to tool around in.

Their most publicized pre-broadcast experience was their meeting with Cassius Clay. The man who would later change his name to Muhammad Ali was in Miami training for his heavyweight championship boxing match with the current champion, Sonny Liston. It was a long, fun-filled encounter highlighted by a mock boxing match in which the future heavyweight champion of the world "knocked out" all four Beatles. Although none of the scores of reporters and photographers present could have realized it, it was a meeting of what would soon become the five most famous and recognizable people in the world.

The Beatles' second appearance on *The Ed Sullivan Show* was to be telecast live from the Deauville's enormous ballroom. On the afternoon of February 16, the band prepared for their performance by rehearsing before a live audience. Then it was time for the show. Once again, more than seventy million people sat glued to their television sets. What none of them had any way of knowing was that first the show and then the Beatles themselves almost did not go on.

The Deauville's ballroom was packed to capacity. Hundreds of young fans had been turned away from watching their idols in person. But a large group of them had noticed the communications truck standing in the hotel's parking lot. Among other broadcasting equipment, it contained the electrical wires connected to the program's television cameras inside the ballroom. The back door to the truck had been left open, and the fans noticed that there were television monitors inside. Realizing this would be a great place to watch the show, they stormed the truck. Just in the nick of time, a man inside the truck shut and locked the door.

Clowning around with Cassius Clay

"They were pushing against the truck and it started to rock," he recalled. "I was worried that the wires would break and electrocute somebody and knock us off the air."

Finally, the crowd realized it could not get into the truck and ran away to find another place to watch the program.

The pre-telecast chaos was far from over. At the same time that the fans were storming the truck, the Beatles were about to enter the ballroom. But as they started to make their way, their path was completely blocked by a huge throng of teens who had failed to gain admission to the show. Almost half of America was waiting to watch them, and yet there was a real possibility that the Beatles would not be able to reach the stage. Hastily, several policemen were summoned, and, forming a human wedge, they carved out a passage through the crowd to the ballroom door.

The show had already begun. As the television cameras rolled, Ed Sullivan was introducing the Beatles. He was in the midst of his introduction when he noticed that none of the four members were in the ballroom. Quickly he signaled to those in the control booth and had them switch to a commercial.

At last, the Beatles entered the ballroom and ran up the aisle. The commercial was just ending when they reached the stage. There was not even time for all their microphones to be properly hooked up. But, within seconds after reaching their instruments, they plugged them in and launched into their first song, "She Loves You." They rounded out their first set with "This Boy" and "All My Loving."

As had been the case with their previous appearance on his show, Sullivan set up the program so that the Beatles both opened and closed it. When they finished their first set, the stage was turned over to a comedy team, a singer/dancer, another comedian, and a group of acrobats. Then the Beatles reappeared, singing "I Saw Her Standing There," "From Me to You," and "I Want to Hold Your Hand," which continued to be the number-one recording in America. When the telecast was over, the Beatles attended a celebration party for the show's staff and performers, given by the Deauville Hotel's owner. Buoyed by this latest American success, John, Paul, and George were in a joyous mood. Ringo, however, seemed downbeat. Asked why he was feeling sad, Ringo replied, "It will never be any better than this."

THE THIRD *ED SULLIVAN SHOW*

The Beatles' live performance on *The Ed Sullivan Show* in Miami was not the final time the band appeared on the program that had launched its conquest of America. Hours before the Fab Four had made their historic February 9, 1964, *Sullivan Show* debut, they had taped two brief segments to be shown on a later program.

Because of the unprecedented success of the February 9 and February 16 Beatles appearances, Sullivan decided to air the taped segments on his February 23 show, making it three consecutive weeks he would feature the world's hottest entertainers.

By the time the February 23 *Ed Sullivan Show* was telecast, the Beatles were already back in England. But in his opening remarks, Sullivan implied that the band was appearing live on the program. "Tonight's show

The Beatles' third appearance on *The Ed Sullivan Show*

again stars the Beatles before their return to England . . . ," he stated. Then, after a pause for commercials, he continued, "You know all of us on the show are so darned sorry, and sincerely sorry that this is the third and thus our last current show with the Beatles because these youngsters from Liverpool, England . . . will leave an imprint with everyone over here who has met them. . . . Let's bring on the Beatles."

To the accompaniment of the shrieks of the teens who had attended the taping of the segments, the Beatles then appeared, singing "Twist and Shout" and then "Please Please Me." After performances by a number of other entertainers, including singers Gordon and Sheila MacRae and Cab Calloway and comedians Dave Barry and Morty Gunty, the Beatles reappeared and concluded the show with "I Want to Hold Your Hand."

Ed Sullivan may have deliberately given the impression that the Beatles were performing live on the program. But he wasn't fooling the thousands of teenage viewers who were keeping up with the Fab Four's every move. They knew that the Beatles were already back in England and that their appearance was taped— not that the fans weren't glued to the show anyway.

The band was back in England when the show aired.

And there was another giveaway. On February 9, 1964, during his introductions to the Beatles' taped performances and his introduction to the program itself, Sullivan had made sure to wear the same suit, but had inadvertently worn a slightly different tie. The most observant of the young Beatles fans took delight in picking this up and sharing it with their fellow Beatles fanatics.

The Fab Four's third appearance on *The Ed Sullivan Show* was actually not the final time that they were seen on the program. During its 1965 American tour, the band stopped by the same studio where the February 9, 1964, program had taken place and taped six songs, which were featured on the September 12, 1965, *Ed Sullivan Show*.

7

HOW THE BEATLES BECAME PRISONERS OF SUCCESS

WE LOVE THE BEATLES

On February 22, 1964, the Beatles returned to England. Less than

four months later, they embarked on their most ambitious concert tour yet, a trip that would take them to Denmark, the Netherlands, Hong Kong, Australia, and New Zealand. Everywhere they appeared, not only at the concerts, but while their plane was refueling or while they were attempting to relax at some supposedly secret hideaway, enormous numbers of fans materialized. This reached a fever pitch when they arrived in Australia. In Melbourne, some 250,000 people, not all of them teenagers, stood chanting for the Beatles outside their hotel. In Adelaide, the throng that gathered outside of where they were staying topped 300,000. When they returned home and traveled to Liverpool to attend a reception for the premiere of *A Hard Day's Night,* more than 100,000 residents of the city where it had all started lined the streets to get a glimpse of their most famous sons. Everywhere they went, the Beatles were now attracting even larger crowds than had turned out to see them in either England or America.

By this time, one of their albums, *Meet the Beatles!,* had sold over four million copies. And Beatlemania was sweeping the world. Stores throughout the globe were filled with Beatles merchandise. There were Beatles record players, record-carrying cases, headphones, and plastic guitars. There were Beatles pillows, shoulder bags, purses, and wallets. There were Beatles sneakers, scarves, socks, and stockings. There was even Beatles bubble bath, shampoo, and hair spray. Among the most popular of all the back-to-school items were Beatles book covers, notebooks, pens, and pencils. And everywhere, John, Paul, George, and Ringo bobble-head and inflatable dolls and Beatles wigs flew off the shelves.

For the Beatles, it was still almost too amazing to comprehend. Yet, despite their unprecedented success, they were beginning to feel something else. They were becoming disenchanted with having to be escorted by police bodyguards, by being trapped in their dressing rooms, by living in what amounted to a fishbowl.

Still it went on. In August 1964, they set out on a gigantic tour of the United States— twenty-four cities, 24,441 miles, thirty performances. The madness intensified. When they landed in Dallas, frenzied fans broke through the police barricades, stormed the plane, and climbed up on its wings. The most hysterical among the crowd began beating at the aircraft's windows with Coke bottles. When they arrived at their Dallas hotel, they were greeted with the news that one of the hotel's maids had been kidnapped and told that she would be physically harmed if she did not reveal just where in the hotel the Beatles were planning to stay. In Seattle, a girl fell off an overhead beam where she had positioned herself, onto the stage, narrowly missing Ringo. In Cleveland, police had to rescue the Fab Four during their performance by throwing a giant net over two hundred fans who had rushed the stage. In Los Angeles, the only way that the band could safely avoid being mauled by the thousands of fans waiting for them to leave the auditorium after their concert was in an armored truck. By the time they had reached Toronto midway through the tour, it had been decided that the only way to bring them into a city undetected was to do so in the wee hours of the morning. This plan didn't solve the

BEATLE FOR A WEEK

The name Jimmy Nicol is largely unknown to even the most avid followers of popular music. Yet Nicol played an important, albeit brief, role in the Beatles' story.

In June 1964, as the Beatles were about to embark on their whirlwind tour of Scandinavia, Holland, the Far East, and Australia, Ringo had to have his tonsils removed. Hastily searching for a replacement, George Martin called in Nicol, who had been a drummer for one group called the Spotnicks and another named the Blue Flames. After rehearsing with John, Paul, and George on the afternoon of June 3, Nicol performed with them in Denmark the following night.

Jimmy Nicol fills in for Ringo.

A week later, when the Beatles reached Australia, Ringo pronounced himself well enough to return to work. Nicol was paid his agreed-upon fee of £500 (In 1963, $1 equaled £0.35, and £500 was equal to approximately $180) and was given a gold watch. He had been a Beatle for only a week. He had performed well and, without realizing it, he had made a lasting contribution.

After every concert the Beatles gave while Nicol was their drummer, Paul would ask him how he felt he was doing. Nicol's answer was always the same. "It's getting better," he would reply. It was a phrase that stuck in Paul's mind. Years later, when he and John were writing their songs for *Sgt. Pepper's Lonely Hearts Club Band*, the phrase came back to him and the song "It's Getting Better" was born and included in the album.

problem since the band's "secret" motorcade passed seventeen miles of continuous parked cars filled with Beatles fans on its way to their hotel.

For the Beatles, the year 1965 would be more of the same. They would, wherever possible, scramble into a studio and make a recording, but it would be another year dominated by touring. It began with a tour of France, Italy, and Spain. It would also include yet another North American tour to ten cities.

By this time, the Fab Four were not only disenchanted with touring, but they were becoming genuinely fearful for their safety. They had begun getting death threats. And, more than ever, they were being unintentionally terrorized by their fans. As had happened elsewhere, when they landed in Houston, hundreds of fans broke through the police barriers and surrounded the plane. Some, including older fans smoking cigarettes, even climbed up on the aircraft's wings so they could wave through the windows at their idols. Only luck prevented a tragic explosion from taking place.

Aside from the adulation and mayhem, the highlight of the 1965 North American Tour would be the Beatles' appearance at New York's Shea Stadium. It would be one of the most famous concerts, not only of its era, but of all time. And it would represent yet another profound and lasting change that the Beatles would bring to the world of popular music. Prior to the Fab Four's appearance at Shea Stadium, the largest crowd ever to attend a rock concert had been twenty thousand people. More than fifty-five thousand Beatles fans showed up at Shea. The event not

John Lennon (seated) and George Harrison in disguise

only shattered the previous concert attendance record, but it set a new type of record as well. "Over 55,000 people saw the Beatles at Shea Stadium," the concert's promoter later exclaimed. "We took [in] $304,000, the greatest gross ever in the history of show business." Along with all the other ways in which the Beatles had revolutionized popular music, they had set the stage for today's megaconcerts by demonstrating that enormous outdoor concerts could be both successful and highly profitable.

The Shea Stadium concert was, in many ways, a colossal triumph. But it was also a verification of what had been deeply disturbing Paul, John, George, and Ringo for a long time. It was more obvious than ever that with all the nonstop screaming that went on as they played, most fans were just interested in the spectacle of a Beatles performance and weren't listening to the actual music they played. At mammoth Shea Stadium it was even worse. The audience was so far away from the makeshift stage that any real connection with the performers was impossible.

Years later, Ringo would reflect upon the feelings he had had during the Shea Stadium appearance. "What I remember most about the concert," he would recall, "is that we were so far away from the audience. . . . When I tour now, I like the audience right in my face. I like to have the reaction, something going on together between me and them. It was just very distant at Shea. Sure, we were big-time, and it was the first time we'd played to thousands and thousands of people, and we were the first band to do it; but it was totally against what we had started out to achieve, which was to entertain right *there*, up close. And screaming had just become the thing to do. We didn't say, 'OK, don't forget, at this concert—everybody scream!' Everybody just screamed."

BEATLES FOR SALE

There were many reasons why the Beatles stopped touring and began to concentrate on making albums in the studio. Among them was their awareness that Beatlemania had gotten out of hand. Even the Beatles themselves had not fully understood how much even a one-night appearance was worth. Nor had they fully appreciated how much value had become attached to almost everything with which they came in contact. A prime example of this took place during their 1965 North American tour. When that tour was arranged, Kansas City was not one of the cities scheduled to host a Beatles concert. This did not sit well with one of its leading citizens, Charles O. Finley. Intent on seeing that his city was not left out, Finley, the millionaire owner of the Kansas City Athletics Major League Baseball team, offered the Beatles the then-princely sum of $100,000 to make a one-night appearance at Kansas City Stadium.

When the Beatles moved on to their next tour stop, two enterprising Chicago businessmen bought sixteen sheets and eight pillowcases that the Fab Four had slept on in their hotel rooms. They cut the unlaundered sheets and pillowcases into three-inch squares, pasted each of the squares onto a card accompanied by a notarized seal verifying that each tiny piece of linen had once touched the body of a Beatle, and sold all the squares at a huge profit. The towels the Beatles had used to wipe the perspiration off their faces during the concert were also cut up and sold.

The sheets, pillowcases, and towels were not the most unusual Beatles merchandise for sale. In New York City another product was enjoying brisk sales. It was canned Beatles' breath.

Beatles' hair for sale

To many of their fans, the historic turnout for the Fab Four at Shea Stadium seemed like the high point of their career thus far. But for the band, it was a confirmation that their days of constant touring had to end. John, in particular, shared George's frustration at playing to audiences who were more intent on seeing them than listening to them. He was also alarmed at the way the four of them, who had been so dedicated to making each performance as perfect as they could, were becoming far less dedicated to rehearsing before setting out on tour. As George stated, "We can't hear ourselves and the fans don't want to listen, so what's the point of bothering?"

There were other reasons for their desire to stop touring as well. More than ever, their physical safety was becoming a real issue. They were never more fearful than when they took the stage in Memphis, Tennessee, their first appearance in the American South. They had made it clear that they would never perform before an audience that was segregated. A Ku Klux Klan official had responded by warning that if they went onstage they would face bodily harm. That night, in the middle of one of their numbers, a firecracker exploded in the auditorium. Ducking for cover, each of the Beatles was certain that someone was firing a rifle at them.

Typical Klu Klux Klan garb

With it all, John had yet another reason for telling Brian Epstein that the touring had to stop.

"People think fame and money bring freedom," he declared, "but they don't.

We're more conscious now of the limitations it places on us rather than the freedom. We can't even spend the allowance we get, because there's nothing to spend it on. What can you spend [it] on in a room? When you're on tour, you exist in this kind of vacuum all the time."

The touring had to end. They all agreed on that. But first, there were existing commitments that had to be met. Chief among them were concerts scheduled for Japan and the Philippines.

As if to accentuate their disenchantment with touring, things in Japan did not go well. Troubles emerged even before they reached that country. Because of a typhoon, their flight was diverted and they were stranded in Alaska for several hours. When they were finally able to resume their flight and reached Japan, they ran into further trouble. The tour's local promoters had arranged for them to give their performance in a majestic hall that was ordinarily used to stage traditional Japanese martial arts demonstrations and contests. What the Beatles and their entourage did not know was that the Japanese people considered the hall sacred. Many were outraged that it was about to be used for a rock concert, complete with shrieking fans.

For the first time, angry demonstrations and marches protesting a Beatles appearance were held. That didn't stop more than ten thousand fans from attending the concert, but the Fab Four were so shaken by the bitter protests that they all later agreed that it was one of their worst performances.

Things got much worse when they moved on to the Philippines. The country was ruled by the dictator Ferdinand Marcos and his wife, Imelda. As a courtesy, the ruling couple and their three children were invited to be honored guests at the two concerts the Beatles were to give in the capitol city of Manila. The two performances were held in Manila's National Football Stadium, with an extraordinary crowd of 50,000 fans in attendance. It should have been the type of success that helped erase the bitter memories of the Japanese experience. But, as in Japan, the Beatles fell victim to circumstances they knew nothing about.

The Marcoses had invited the band to attend a party for their children at the royal palace. But the band had never been told of the invitation. The morning after the concert, newspapers throughout the Philippines headlined angry stories about how the Beatles had snubbed their nation's leaders. The country erupted in outrage. Personnel at the British embassy in Manila and the Beatles received death threats. The local promoter of the concerts refused to pay the Fab Four for their performances. When Brian Epstein made arrangements for the Beatles to go on television and explain what had happened, the transmission of their apology was halted by mysterious technical difficulties.

And it got even worse. When the time finally came for them to leave the Philippines, the Beatles discovered that the authorities had abruptly removed their security guards. When they left their hotel and again when they arrived at the airport, the group adored by much of the world was jostled, kicked, and even punched. It didn't help that, as soon as they were in the air, President Marcos released a statement explaining that the Beatles had not intentionally stood up the dictator and his wife.

For the Beatles, the horrific experiences in Japan and the Philippines removed any doubts they had about ending touring. They still had one final North American trip to get through. But by August 29, 1966, when they arrived to give the tour's last concert at San Francisco's Candlestick Park, their decision had been firmly made. "We'd done about 1,400 live shows and I certainly felt [the Candlestick Park concert] was it . . . ," George later stated. "It was nice to be popular, but when you saw the size of it,

A Beatles boycott in the Philippines led to a rare sight—empty seats.

it was ridiculous, and it felt dangerous because everybody was out of hand and out of line. Even the cops were out of line. . . . It was a very strange feeling. For a year or so I'd been saying, 'Let's not do this anymore.' And then it played itself out, so that by 1966 everybody was feeling, 'We've got to stop this.' I don't know exactly where in 1966, but obviously after the Philippines we thought, 'Hey we've got to pack this in.'"

When the Candlestick Park performance was over, the Beatles took their final bows. Then they each grabbed a camera and took pictures of themselves onstage. They had never done this before, but it seemed to be a fitting way to commemorate their last concert. It was the end of four years in the life of the most popular music group the world had ever known. What they had no way of realizing was that their greatest successes—and, more important, their greatest contributions to the world—still lay ahead.

The Beatles are sourrounded by unruly fans at
their final concert, at Candlestick Park

8

HOW THE BEATLES CHANGED FASHION

The Beach Boys' hair and clothing were more typical of American style before the Beatles.

When they arrived in America to appear on *The Ed Sullivan Show*, the Beatles astounded the nation, not only with their music, but with their physical appearance, particularly their hair. At a time when the accepted haircut for men was above the ears, and crew cuts and flattops were common, the Beatles' hair was shockingly long and unusual looking. Young fans loved the look, but their parents were shocked. Many adults were outraged, regarding the hairstyle as a dangerous sign of youthful rebellion.

The Beatles' hair, in fact, became as much a topic of conversation as their music. During their first pre–*Ed Sullivan Show* press conference, John, Paul, George, and Ringo were asked more questions about their hair than about their songs or their style of performing them. The Beatles replied with their usual wit. Asked by a reporter, "What do you call your hairstyle?" George sent the room into gales of laughter by answering, "Arthur!"

The Fab Four had acquired what would become known around the world as the "Beatles hairdo" while they had been performing in Hamburg. While there, they had met a young, talented photographer named Astrid Kirchherr, who had become Stu Sutcliffe's girlfriend. One day, deciding that Sutcliffe needed a makeover, Kirchherr had cut his hair. The haircut that Kirchherr gave Sutcliffe left his hair long and combed downward. It was a hairstyle that Germans called *pilzkopf,* meaning "mushroom head" or what English-speaking observers called "mophead."

Almost as a lark, John, Paul, George, and Ringo got themselves similar haircuts. At first they were taken aback by what they now looked like. But they soon decided that the mop-top hairstyle had real advantages. "We nearly tried to change it back," Paul would later explain, "but it wouldn't go, it kept flapping forward. And that just caught on.

"We weren't really into the [hairstyle]. It was like [Moe's] out of the Three Stooges.

It fell forward in a fringe. But it was great for us because we never had to style it or anything—wash it, towel it, turn upside down, and give it a shake and that was it. Everyone thought we had started it, so it became 'the Beatle hairdo.'"

The trademark hairstyle of what would become the most popular band the world had ever

Boys everywhere began to copy the Beatles' hairdo.

known would change the way millions of men would wear their hair. Thanks to the Beatles' extraordinary popularity, for the first time in centuries, men worldwide began letting their hair grow down over their ears. For many of these men, long hair became a symbol of rebellion against customary fashion. For others, it was simply a bold new way of presenting themselves.

The manner in which they changed hairstyles was far from the only way the Beatles had a profound effect on fashion. By the time the Fab Four were into their first American tour in 1964, they had also brought about a profound change in the type of footwear that many men wore.

In late 1961, at the time that Brian Epstein was transforming the Beatles' image by having them switch from leather attire to suits, they discovered a special type of boots that they felt would handsomely complement their new outfits. Called Chelsea boots, they were ankle high and tight fitting. One of their distinctive features was a seam stitch that ran down the center, from the top of the boots to their sharp-pointed toes. Epstein and the Fab Four customized the footwear by having a shoe company remove their customary heels and replace them with what were known as Cuban heels, which, while moderate in height, were broader than most boot heels and slightly tapered in the back.

As an integral part of the Beatles' new look, their boots became so admired and popular with their male fans that they quickly became known as Beatles boots. They were adopted not only by Beatles

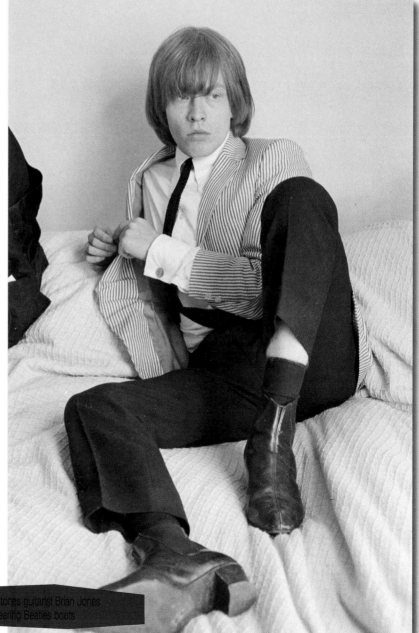

Rolling Stones guitarist Brian Jones wearing Beatles boots

admirers but by competing musical groups as well. By the middle of the 1970s, one would have been hard-pressed to find a rock-and-roll performer who was not shod in Beatles boots.

Today, the footwear made so popular by the Fab Four remains a commonly advertised article of apparel on the Internet, making Beatles boots one of the most enduring ways the Beatles changed the world of fashion.

Yet another Beatles fashion innovation, one that also remains in great evidence today, was initiated not by the band as a group, but individually by one of the Fab Four. In 1966, John took a break from the Beatles and starred in a movie titled *How I Won the War*. As part of his wardrobe for the film, the directors gave him a special type of eyeglasses to wear. Round and thin-framed, they were called teashade glasses. John liked the way they looked on him so much that he made them a permanent part of his appearance. Because of his enormous visibility and popularity, it was not long before men everywhere began to wear the same type of spectacles, which became known as John Lennon glasses.

Their popularity and their historical significance was particularly evident in 2007, when a pair of the glasses that John himself had worn was put up for auction. One would not ordinarily expect a pair of spectacles to fetch a hefty price. But, as one of the auction officials stated at the time, "Our phones have been in meltdown since the announcement of the auction ... with a ferocious bidding war breaking out around the globe."

By the time the bidding war ended, one of John's original pairs of glasses sold for almost $2 million.

Had the Beatles' influence on fashions ended with their earliest contributions, they still would have had an enormous impact on what became fashionable from their time until today. But, from the start, the Fab Four kept reinventing their look along with their music. They had started by revolutionizing men's fashions with their long hair, Edwardian-era suits, and unique boots. In 1966, they helped spawn a whole new fashion trend when they began wearing more casual clothes, including blue jeans, T-shirts, and denim jackets.

In 1967 and 1968, at the same time they were experimenting with their music and producing groundbreaking albums, the Beatles experimented with their clothing as well. The result was the most dramatic of all their fashion transformations. In keeping with what became known as the psychedelic era, they turned to wearing brightly colored suits and shirts with floral patterns. They also wore and popularized clothing based on traditional ways of dress in India.

Thanks to the Beatles' so-called peacock style of presenting themselves, another dramatic change took place. For the first time, men began to display a flair for fashion, which had for so long been the exclusive domain of women.

And it was not only their wardrobe that kept changing. At different times, the Fab Four adopted various types of facial hair, including mustaches and bushy beards. They kept changing the length of their hair as well. All these changes were adopted by legions of men.

The various profound effects the Beatles had on fashion continued even after they split apart. One of the reasons for their breakup would be their desire to pursue individual lives and different lifestyles. These choices would be reflected in their clothing. Ringo would become more dapper, even flamboyant in his dress. Paul would eventually embrace a clean-cut, casual look. George matched his style of dress to the Indian philosophy he adopted. John would continue to constantly change his fashion style.

As with all else they transformed, the Beatles were well aware of the changes in fashion they continually brought about. As John proudly proclaimed,

"We changed the hairstyles and clothes of the world, including America—they were a very square and sorry lot when we went over."

The Beatles helped set off a men's fashion revolution.

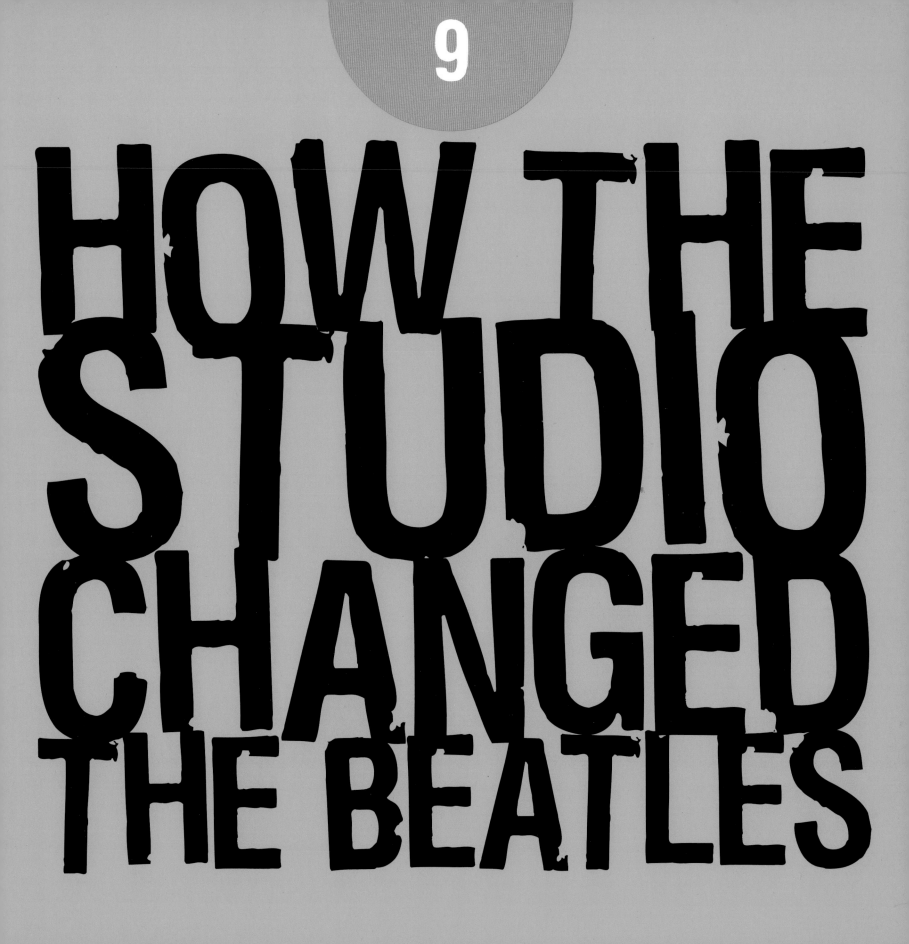

9

HOW THE STUDIO CHANGED THE BEATLES

Ringo Starr and George Harrison arrive at the EMI
recording studios on Abbey Road.

For the Beatles, the end of touring brought a

tremendous sense of relief. It meant the end of constant days on the road; the end of being continually trapped in limousines, hotels, and dressing rooms; the end of performing songs that could not be heard over the shrieks and cries of their hysterical fans. But they were each feeling something else as well. Paul put it simply. "We'd had our cute period," he stated, "and now it was time to expand."

As George Martin, who was personally guiding the production of their records and albums, would later explain, "The Beatles didn't get totally immersed in record production until . . .

they stopped touring. Until then, they didn't have time." Now they could spend weeks, even months at a stretch, composing and recording, going deeper, blazing new trails, creating new and more meaningful forms of music. And blaze new trails they did, further revolutionizing the world of popular music.

Actually, the Beatles had already gotten a taste of what having a long stretch of time to compose and record could mean. Toward the end of their touring days they had found themselves with more than a month between concert bookings. For the first time, they could spend long, uninterrupted hours at Abbey Road, their recording studio, experimenting with new sounds and new approaches to their work. The result was *Rubber Soul*, a work George Martin would call "the first of the albums that presented a new Beatles to the world. Up to this point," Martin would explain, "we had been making albums that were rather like a collection of their singles, and now we really were beginning to think about albums as a bit of art in their own right. We were thinking about the album as an entity of its own, and *Rubber Soul* was the first one to emerge in this way."

That album would become yet another commercial success for the Beatles. But it would be much more than that. It would be, as *Rolling Stone* magazine would describe it, "a stunning collection" that introduced the Beatles' "newfound sophistication and depth." The album would include the song "Drive My Car," the group's first comic character study. It would contain highly emotional songs, such as "You Can't See Me" and "I'm Looking Through You." The band's desire to experiment with new instrumentation was seen in the song "Norwegian Wood," in which George was featured playing the sitar, the first time that an Indian instrument had ever

George Harrison receiving sitar lessons.

been used in a pop song. Most importantly, the band's determination to become more serious and personal in their songwriting was evidenced by John's motivation for writing "Nowhere Man."

After struggling for more than five hours to complete "Nowhere Man," John began to believe he would never finish it. "I'd actually stopped trying to think of something," he later told an interviewer. "Nothing would come. I was [upset] and went for a lie-down, having given up. Then I thought of myself as Nowhere Man—sitting in his nowhere land."

Later, George would call *Rubber Soul* "the best [album] we made." One of the reasons, he would state, was because "we were suddenly hearing sounds that we weren't able to hear before." More important was the way they brought a whole new dimension to the world of albums. The way in which their albums began to present a story, rather than being simply a collection of songs, was not only revolutionary, but startling even to those in the music industry. As the Beach Boys' Brian Wilson, a highly respected songwriter and rock star in his own right, would state, "We prayed for an album that would be a rival to *Rubber Soul*."

Almost without exception, music critics agreed that *Rubber Soul* was a "major artistic achievement," and one that revealed the Beatles' developing musical vision.

The Beatles continued their experimentation and their growth as musical artists with their next album, titled *Revolver*. In many ways it was an adventurous extension of *Rubber Soul*. As George would say, "To me, they could be Volume One and Volume Two." But the album included its own special innovations. Perhaps most notable was John's rendition of "Tomorrow Never Knows," in which he deliberately brought a deeply spiritual quality to the song.

Revolver also included "Eleanor Rigby," a song that led Jerry Lieber, the songwriter of such rock-and-roll classics as "Hound Dog" and "Jailhouse Rock" to state, "I don't think there has ever been a better song written than 'Eleanor

The innovative *Revolver* album cover

Rigby.'" With its focus on death and loneliness, the song was a prime example of how, in the words of *Rolling Stone*, "*Revolver* signaled that in popular music, anything—any theme, any musical idea—could now be realized."

Another of the album's important innovations had nothing to do with its music but with its package. During their days in Hamburg, the Beatles had struck up a friendship with artist Klaus Voormann. At Martin's and the Beatles' urging, Voormann created a dramatic photo collage for the *Revolver* cover, which would further revolutionize the way that albums would be presented.

No one was more impressed with what the Beatles were accomplishing in the studio than George Martin. "At the start, I thought . . . this can't last forever," he would write. "They've given me so much great stuff that I can't expect them to keep doing it." But to his surprise, the Beatles not only kept doing it, they followed *Revolver* by creating what *Rolling Stone* has called "the most important rock-and-roll album ever made, an unsurpassed adventure in concept, sound, songwriting, cover art and studio technology."

Beatles in their Sgt. Pepper costumes

The name of the album itself was both innovative and intriguing. It was called *Sgt. Pepper's Lonely Hearts Club Band*, and it was Paul's idea. On a flight back from a brief vacation in Kenya, he found himself thinking about how he'd had to wear a disguise to travel undetected earlier in his trip. He began to consider the idea of the Beatles creating an album in which they would all be in disguise. "It liberated you," he would later explain. "You could do anything when you got to the mic or on your guitar, because it wasn't you."

Years later, after the album had been made and had become the bestselling album up to that time, several theories would be put forth as to the origin of such a unique album title. One of the most common speculations was that it was derived from the popular soft drink Dr Pepper.

GEORGE MARTIN

From the time he entered the music business, George Martin demonstrated an extraordinary ability and versatility as a record producer, musical arranger, composer, and musician. With thirty number-one hit singles in Great Britain and twenty-three number-one hits in the United States among his scores of other achievements, he is widely regarded as one of the greatest record producers of all time.

For more than sixty years, Martin brought his talents to music, movies, television, and live performance. He would gain his greatest fame through his association with the Beatles. As a record-company executive, he first met the group on June 6, 1962, where they auditioned for him, seeking a recording contract. The Beatles did not overwhelm Martin with their audition performance. But when he asked them what they thought needed to be changed, George Harrison immediately replied, "Well, there's your tie, for a start." John and Paul joined in with witticisms of their own. At this point, more impressed with the young men's humor than their playing, Martin signed them to their first recording contract.

It did not take Martin long to discover that the Beatles had far more going for them than simply their wit. On November 26, 1962, the group recorded their song "Please Please Me" for him. When they finished, Martin made a bold pronouncement. "Gentlemen," he told them, "you have just made your first number-one record."

John and Paul had written "Please Please Me" as a slow ballad. But when the Beatles recorded it, Martin continually urged them to speed up their playing of the song. It was a vital contribution to the record's success. And, as the Beatles would quickly discover, it would be only the beginning of what Martin's contributions would mean to the group.

The vast majority of the Beatles' singles and albums were made under Martin's guidance. He created many of the musical arrangements for their songs and conducted the music for many of their recordings. And he championed the experimentation and innovation that came to characterize their music and lyrics. As Paul, with typical Beatle wit, declared, "George Martin [was] quite experimental for who he was, a grown-up."

Martin's achievements extended well beyond all he had accomplished with the Beatles. Among many other achievements, he produced two main theme songs for the highly popular James Bond motion picture series. Both of them, "Goldfinger" and "Live and Let Die," remain two of the most recognizable movie themes of all time. In 1996, in recognition of all he had contributed, he was knighted by England's Queen Elizabeth II. A year

George Martin and Paul McCartney

later, shortly after Princess Diana's untimely death, he produced Elton John's "Candle in the Wind 1997," a record that became the bestselling single of all time. Fittingly, George Martin's final recording production was a project titled *In My Life*, a collection of Beatles songs.

The impact of *Sgt. Pepper* lives on in a tribute at the London Olympics Opening Ceremony in 2012.

But Paul himself would set the record straight. "It was at the start of the hippy times," he would explain, "and there was a jingly-jangly happy aura all around. . . . I started thinking about what would be a really mad name to call a band. At the time there were lots of groups with names like 'Laughing Joe and His Medicine Band' or 'Col Tucker's Medicinal Brew and Compound' . . . with long rambling names. And so . . . I threw those words together: 'Sgt. Pepper's Lonely Hearts Club Band.' I took an idea back to the guys in London . . . how about if we become an alter-ego band, something like say 'Sgt. Pepper's Lonely Hearts'? I've got a little bit of a song cooking with that title."

When he returned to the London studio, Paul shared the song he was writing with the rest of the group. Without hesitation, they decided to create an album around it, an album about an imaginary concert by a fictitious band played by the Beatles. It would be an extraordinary endeavor. By this time, the Fab Four were totally caught up in experimentation, constantly pushing and challenging each other, continually working and reworking their songs and how they recorded them.

"*Sgt. Pepper* was our grandest endeavor," Ringo would later declare. **"It gave everybody—including me—a lot of leeway to come up with ideas and to try different material . . . .**

The great thing about the band was that whoever had the best idea (it didn't matter who), that would be the one we'd use. No one was standing on their ego, saying, 'Well, it's mine,' and getting possessive. Always, the best was used. That's why the standard of the songs always remained high . . ."

It would take an unprecedented seven hundred hours to create the *Sgt. Pepper's Lonely Hearts Club Band* album. Several of its songs would become among the most memorable ever written, including "Lucy in the Sky with Diamonds," "When I'm Sixty-Four," "A Day in the Life," and "Strawberry Fields Forever." Hailing *Sgt. Pepper* as an extraordinary advance even in the tremendous progress of the Beatles, the music critic for London's *Sunday Times* noted that the words to many of the songs were "splendid . . . poetry—almost metaphysical."

As in *Rubber Soul* and *Revolver, Sgt. Pepper* was characterized by the Beatles' determination to bring innovation to every aspect of the album. Along with employing experimental recording techniques, in several songs the Beatles were accompanied by a full orchestra. Also innovative was the wide range of songs the album contained, including rock and roll, pop, traditional British music hall melodies, and Indian music. Building on the precedent that had been set with *Revolver, Sgt. Pepper's Lonely Hearts Club Band* had an even more striking album cover, depicting the Beatles in elaborate marching-band uniforms, surrounded by an identifiable audience of historical figures. The significance of the lyrics led to another innovation. *Sgt. Pepper* became the first rock-and-roll album ever to include printed lyrics to all its songs, another feature that the pop-music world would soon adopt.

Sgt. Pepper's Lonely Hearts Club Band was released in June 1967. And it caused a sensation. "Nothing remotely like *Pepper* had been heard before," George Martin stated. "It came at a time when people were thirsty for something new, but its newness still caught them by surprise . . . With *Pepper* [the Beatles] drew a line and crossed it."

The album also burst upon the world at a remarkable time in history. The summer of 1967 would become known as the "Summer of Love." It was a time of great social change, caused by the changing youth culture and a season of hope, optimism, and upheaval. Throughout the globe, *Sgt. Pepper's Lonely Hearts Club Band* would become the anthem of this extraordinary period.

Hippie wedding

As *Rolling Stone* magazine has stated, "No other pop record of that era, or since, has had such an immediate, titanic impact."

For the Beatles, *Sgt. Pepper* would be the epitome of what they would accomplish in the studio. With all they created there, they would change both the world of music and the world itself. Not only would they transform popular music but they would change how the public—adults as well as young people—regarded pop stars.

That, perhaps, is their greatest musical contribution of all. Because of the Beatles' willingness to continually experiment and create popular songs that dealt with emotions such as despair or insecurity as well as love and happiness, people around the world began to regard pop music in a whole new way. As author Ellen Willis has written, "Since *Sgt. Pepper,* few people deny that serious pop is serious art."

And, as a result, the Beatles themselves would be profoundly changed. As Paul would declare, "We were [now] not boys, we were men . . . artists rather than performers."

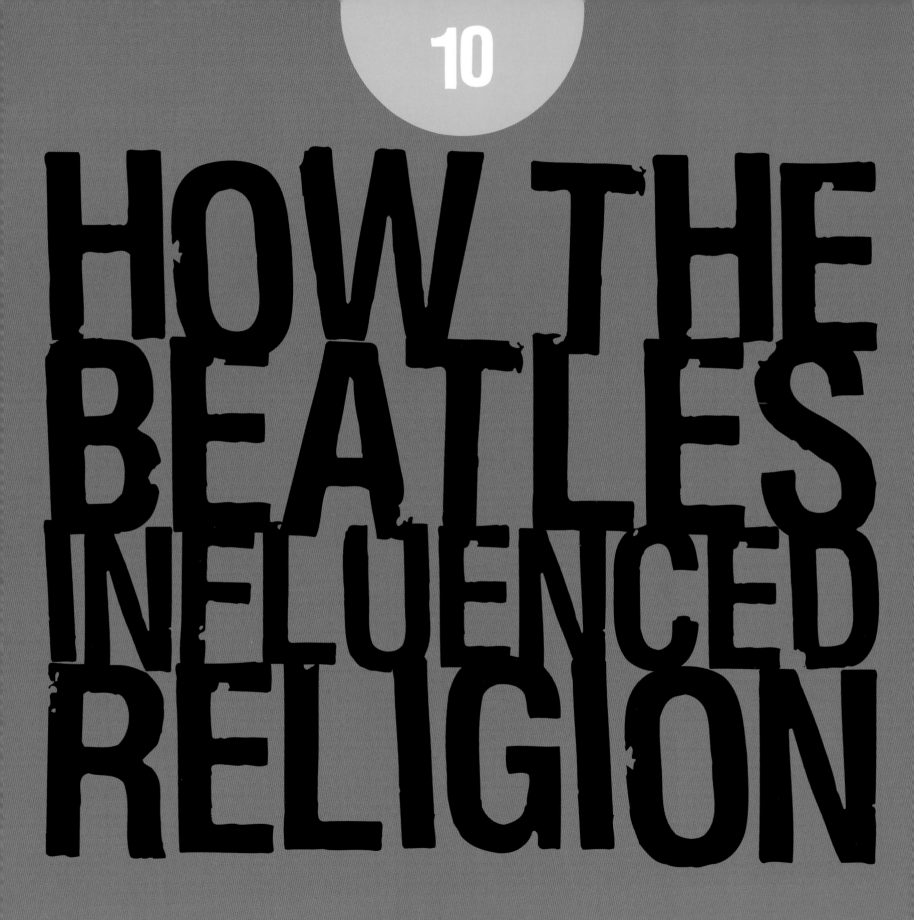

10

HOW THE BEATLES INFLUENCED RELIGION

American teenagers protest against the Beatles.

In March 1966, John was interviewed

by the well-known *London Evening Standard* journalist Maureen Cleave. The interview was supposed to focus on John's assessment of the Beatles and their music. But in the middle of the session, Cleave asked John a most unexpected question. What, she asked, were his thoughts on religion? In his answer, John made the comment, "We're more popular than Jesus now."

It was an offhand remark that went unnoticed in England. But five months later, as the Beatles were about to embark on their third North American tour, and final tour ever, Cleave's interview was reprinted in the American teen magazine *Datebook*. The magazine not only reprinted John's remark; it headlined it on its cover.

Datebook's cover and its article misquoted John as having said that the Beatles were *bigger* that Jesus, which caused an enormous uproar in America, particularly in that area of the South known as the Bible Belt. Throughout the region, ministers spoke out against the Beatles from their pulpits, Beatles music was banned from local radio stations, and huge bonfires were held in which Beatles' merchandise was burned. When on this occasion Ku Klux Klan members threatened the band with bodily harm, the North American tour came close to being canceled.

In the end, the Beatles decided to go forward with the tour. During it, John met with the American press and apologized for his offhand remark. "I just said what I said and it was wrong, or was taken wrong, and now it's all this!" he stated. The apology did much to clear the air, but the anguish the comment had caused John and all of the Beatles would not easily be forgotten.

Actually, the only band member who had ever given much thought to religion was George. The man who would come to be known as "the mystical Beatle" had been profoundly influenced by visits to India, where he had developed what would be a lifelong love of Eastern music and philosophy, particularly its emphasis on spiritual matters. As author Steve Turner has written, "George [came to the understanding] that the only worthwhile pursuit was the search for the answers to the questions, who am I? why am I here? and where am I going? 'We made our money and fame, but for me that wasn't it,' he said. 'It was good fun for a while, but it certainly wasn't the answer to what life is about.'"

George Harrison with Hare Krishnas

It would be through George, or more precisely, his wife, Patti, that the rest of the Beatles would add a religious dimension to their lives. Like George, Patti Harrison was intrigued by Indian culture and religious beliefs, particularly its emphasis on meditation. When she heard that India's most popular guru, the maharishi Mahesh Yogi, was in London delivering a series of lectures in August 1967, she urged all four of the Beatles to accompany her to one of his talks.

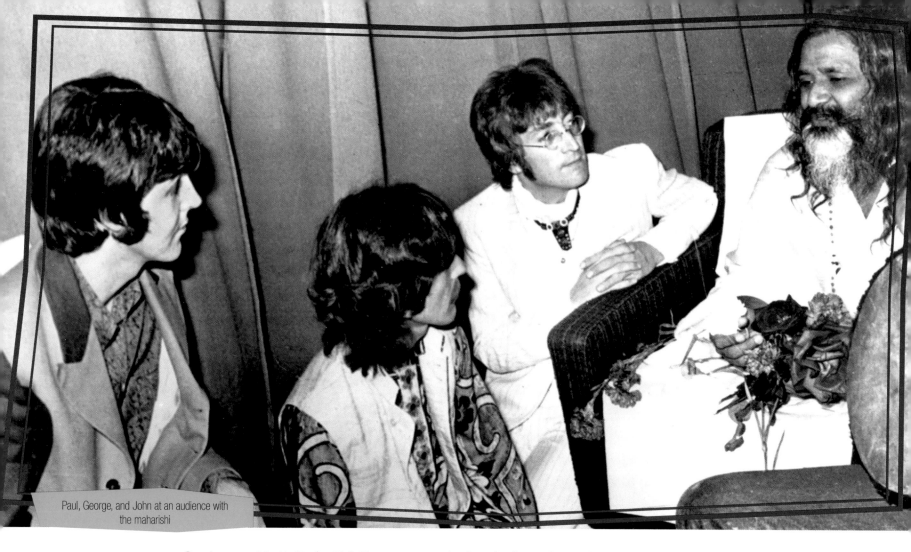

Paul, George, and John at an audience with the maharishi

On August 24, 1967, the Fab Four went to the hotel where the maharishi was giving the final lecture of his London stay. What they didn't know was that the maharishi was a fan of theirs. He had first come to admire them when he had heard that during their first *Ed Sullivan Show* appearance, crime in America had come to a standstill. "It was at this point," the maharishi had said, "that I knew the Beatles were angels on earth."

When the Beatles arrived at the maharishi's lecture, they were given honored seats in the first row. When the talk was over, the guru invited them to meet with him personally in his hotel suite. During the ninety-minute meeting, the maharishi invited them to come to Wales, where, two days later, he was going to begin conducting a ten-day course on the basics of transcendental meditation. Without hesitation, all four Beatles accepted the invitation.

Soon after they had begun taking the course, however, their stay in Wales was cut short when they received the tragic news of Brian Epstein's untimely death. Quickly, they packed their belongings and flew home to attend their manager's funeral. But all through their time back in London, thoughts of the maharishi and his teachings stayed with them. They had met him at a time when each of them was becoming dissatisfied with all the trappings that went along with being a Beatle. As Ringo would state, "The four of us have had the most hectic lives.

The Beatles talk to the media about Brian Epstein's shocking death.

We have got almost anything that money can buy. But when you can do that, the things you buy mean nothing after a time. You look for something else, for a new experience."

For the Fab Four, given how impressed they had been by the maharishi, a "new experience" meant delving deeper into his teachings. For George, not surprisingly, it carried with it a sense of urgency. "Everything else can wait," he would state, "but the search for God cannot wait."

Together the Beatles made an important decision. With wives, girlfriends, and assistants they would travel to the maharishi's fourteen-acre compound in Rishikesh, India, to receive intensive personal training from him in the art of meditation, in the skill of yoga, and in the ancient teachings of Hinduism, one of the most philosophical religions in the world. Like everything else connected with the band, it was a decision that drew enormous public attention. On the day in February 1968 when they arrived at the London train station to begin their journey, they were greeted by hordes of reporters and fans. In its report of their departure, the London-based *Daily Mirror* described the train they boarded as a "Mystical Special."

From the moment they reached their destination, each of the Beatles became immersed in attending lectures by the maharishi. They spent hours in meditation. And each of them was given private lessons by the guru.

There was no question that the Beatles were benefiting from the rare peace and tranquillity they were discovering in India. But their stay with the maharishi would turn out to be much shorter than they had planned. Ringo's wife simply could not stand the swarms of mosquitoes, spiders, and flies that were part and parcel of the Indian environment. Both she and Ringo discovered that they could not tolerate the unfamiliar Indian food. And they both found them-selves missing their children more every day. Despite the fact that Ringo felt himself seriously changed for the better, particularly by the meditation skills he had learned, the couple abruptly left for home on March 1. Slightly more than two weeks later, Paul, who felt that he was ignoring pressing responsibilities back home, particularly the Beatles' newly formed Apple Corporation, also left. But he too felt that he had undergone an important transformation. "I'm a new man," he told one of the maharishi's other students.

John and George stayed on for about six weeks after Paul headed home. But, for what they regarded as serious reasons, they too then departed. Although John was quick to acknowledge that through meditation he had added an important new dimension to his life, he and George both became disenchanted with the maharishi's behavior. Both felt that, as a spiritual leader, he was much too interested in gaining celebrity and money. Most serious of their concerns was the fact that they were convinced that the guru had acted inappropriately with some of his female students.

The Beatles' journey to India would be the last time that the Fab Four would travel abroad together. Despite their abrupt departure, a new door had been opened to them. Meditation would remain an important part of their lives. So too would the practice of yoga. And they had reaped another great benefit from their time there as well.

Undoubtedly influenced by both the tranquillity and the religious surroundings, they became extraordinarily creative. They had, in fact, found the time and the inspiration to write more than thirty new songs, some of them obviously influenced by Eastern music. Some of these songs would become part of the Beatles' *White Album*. Others would be included in *Abbey Road*. Still others would become hit singles. As John would later state, "I was going humity-humity

John found musical inspiration through meditation while in Rishikesh, India.

in my head and the songs were coming out. For creating it was great. It was just pouring out!" Ringo, as well, found creative inspiration in Rishikesh. While there, he wrote "Don't Pass Me By," the first song he had ever written alone, which became a hit.

George would later apologize to the maharishi for the Beatles' abrupt departure from his compound and for the way in which some of their negative remarks about the guru had found

Yoga and meditation have become more popular, thanks in part to the Beatles' early and continued support.

their way into the press. Most important, he and John and Ringo would take time out of their busy schedules to spread the word about the benefits of meditation. The simple fact that the Beatles had embraced the practice as a means to reduce stress and seek inner peace had brought it unprecedented attention. As author Stephanie Syman has documented, after the Beatles began to actively promote meditation, attendance at lectures demonstrating meditation techniques tripled. Asked if the Beatles were deliberately using their power to convince people to begin meditating, John answered, "Yes, because we never felt like this about anything else. We

Paul and Ringo perform at the David Lynch Foundation's "Change Begins Within" show, 2009.

want the younger generation, especially, to know about it. . . . We've got to convince people . . . that what we can do, anyone can do."

The Beatles would continue to promote the benefits of meditation for the rest of their careers. John would extol its virtues on television talk shows. In 1992, George would give a benefit concert for an organization associated with the maharishi. And in 2009, in New York City's jam-packed Radio City Music Hall, Paul and Ringo would reunite to headline a concert in support of introducing meditation programs into schools.

To the ways in which they had changed the worlds of music, movies, and fashion, the Beatles would add the enormous impact they had for inspiring people to search for inner peace and spiritual meaning. Steve Turner put it best. "It is not surprising to me," he wrote, "that the Beatles sought out wonder, meaning, and innocence in their lives and music and that a huge international audience looked to them to find much the same thing."

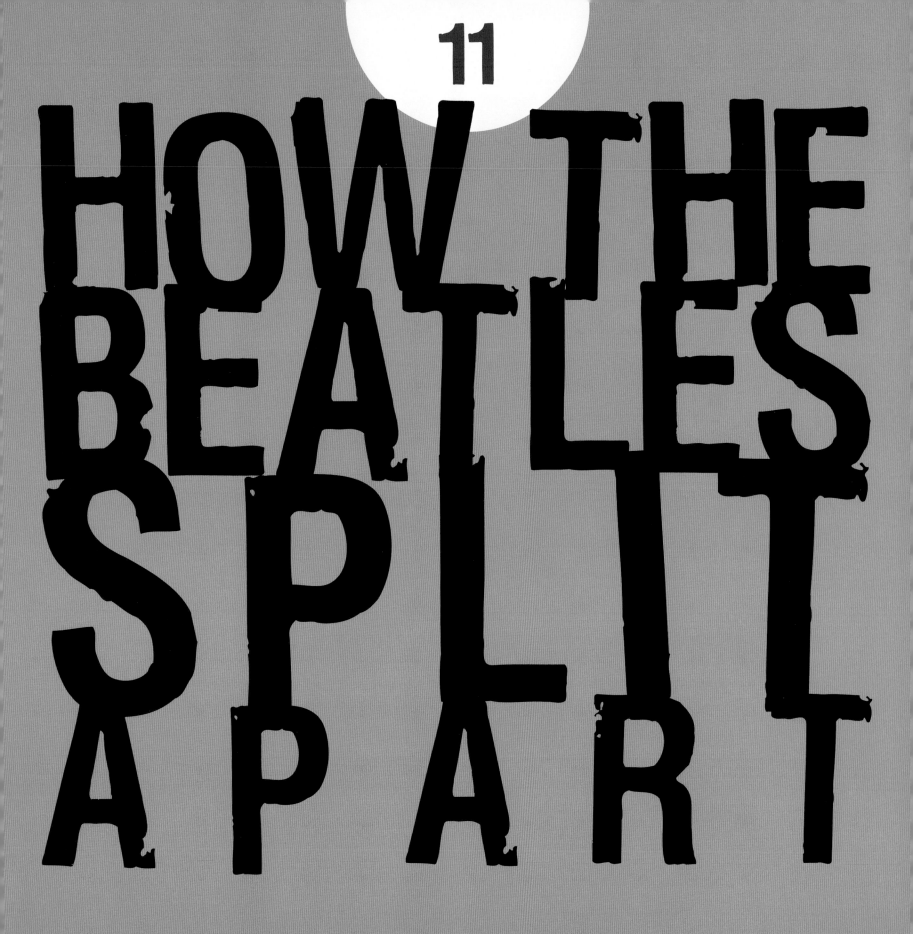

11

HOW THE BEATLES SPLIT APART

John Lennon and Yoko Ono

With the extraordinary creative and sales success

they had achieved in the studio, the Beatles were riding higher than ever. But unknown to their adoring public, things were about to change. "It was getting a bit fraught between us . . . because we'd been together a long time and cracks were beginning to appear," Paul later recounted. John was aware of the budding tensions as well. "We were together much longer than the public knew us," he would state. "It wasn't just from '64. I was twenty-four in '64 and I'd been playing with Paul since I was fifteen and George about a year later. So it's a long time we spent together, in the most extraordinary circumstances, from lousy rooms to great rooms.

It takes a lot to live with four people over and over for years and years, which is what we did. We'd called each other every name under the sun . . . [we'd] been through the mill together for more than ten years."

As Paul had pointed out, the Beatles were no longer boys, but men. And each, after spending so many years together in the same pursuits, wanted to explore different interests. George, the most spiritual of the Fab Four, had developed a passion for India and its religious music. John, who was divorced from his first wife, had fallen in love with a talented Japanese-born artist named Yoko Ono. It was becoming clear that he wanted more and more time alone with her. Ringo, who had developed into the greatest homebody of the group, seemed content to spend as much time as he could with his wife and children. Paul, it seemed, was the only one intent on keeping the group as closely together as it had previously been.

Of all the Beatles, it was John who felt most strongly that the band's days were numbered. For him, this feeling had come to a head when, on August 27, 1967, Brian Epstein died at the age of thirty-two from an overdose of sleeping pills.

Brian Epstein's untimely death destabilized the band.

"The Beatles," John would later declare, "were finished when Eppy died. I knew, deep inside me, that that was it. Without him, we'd had it."

In May 1968, the Beatles went into the studio again to record yet another album. It was simply titled *The Beatles* but would become known as *The White Album* because when it was released, its plain white cover had no illustrations or words on it other than the band's name. Paul had hoped that by returning to the studio, the tensions that had developed within the band would begin to disappear. Instead, discord within the group during the recording sessions drove the Beatles further apart. As the work progressed, John began to feel that, with Epstein

A NOT-SO-MAGICAL TOUR

The sudden death of Brian Epstein was a major blow to the Beatles. Coming at a time when tensions within the band were mounting, the loss of the man who had guided them to their extraordinary success threatened to widen the rift that had developed within the group. Anxious to restore harmony, Paul decided that embarking on a new project would be the answer. And he came up with a new idea. The Beatles would create a television film by piling into a bus accompanied by colorful characters, including clowns and dancers. The bus would travel the English countryside while the television cameramen aboard would record the adventures the band and their companions would be sure to have.

There was to be no script for the made-for-TV film. No one was to have any idea of where he or she was going or what they were going to do. It would be called *Magical Mystery Tour* and, aside from six new Beatles songs, it would all be improvised.

It was an innovative idea, but it didn't work. When it was aired by the BBC at Christmas, the ten hours of film that took eleven weeks to edit into the one-hour movie was a major disappointment. The film attracted some fifteen million viewers. But the critics were almost unanimous in describing the film as chaotic and well below the quality and innovation normally expected from the Fab Four.

Paul's idea for bringing the Beatles closer together had backfired. There had obviously been nothing magical in the *Magical Mystery Tour.*

The bus used to film the *Magical Mystery Tour* TV film

gone, Paul was trying to take control. Ringo had his own problems. Believing that his opinions were being ignored, he abruptly quit the band. He would be coaxed back a short time later with the promise that he would be more included in the group's decisions, but while he was gone, Paul had to play the drums on two of the album's songs. The fact that, for the first time, many of *The White Album*'s songs were sung solo rather than by the group was further evidence that the group was drifting apart.

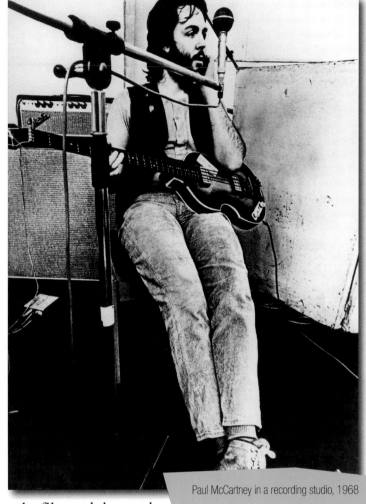

Paul McCartney in a recording studio, 1968

Yet, despite the growing rift, on January 2, 1969, the Beatles were back in the studio again, this time to begin work on a double project, one designed to be both a film of the group making a live album and the album itself. Initially intended to be called *Get Back,* its name would eventually be changed to *Let It Be.*

Later the group would admit that taking on the project only eleven weeks after experiencing so much dissension during their completion of *The White Album* had not been a good idea. But Paul had been persuasive in getting them to do it. He was convinced that by creating the film and the result-ing album in front of a live audience, the Beatles would rediscover the harmony that had, for so long, existed between them.

And for a very brief time they did. By the end of January 1969, they had decided that they needed a special place to end the live film. They chose a most unlikely spot. They decided that, unannounced, they would perform the film's final songs from the roof of the recording studio. "We went on the roof," George would explain, "... to resolve the live concert idea, because it was much simpler than going anywhere else; also nobody had ever done that, so it would be inter-esting to see what happened when we started playing up there." Paul would have his own recol-lections of why the rooftop was chosen. "We'd been looking for an end to the film," Paul would

recall, "and it was a
case of, 'How are we going to
finish this . . . ?' So it was suggested that we
go up on the roof and do a concert there; then we could all go
home. I'm not sure who suggested it. I could say it seems like one of my half-baked ideas, but I'm not sure."

It may, at first, have seemed like a "half-baked" notion, but it turned out to be spectacular. At lunchtime on January 30, the Beatles staged their rooftop concert. As soon as they started playing, they caught the attention of people in neighboring buildings and people passing by on the street. These spectators were treated to an incredible sight. "With the wind sweeping the roof and blowing through the Beatles' hair," one publication would later write, "it seemed as if the roof concert were occurring on ship deck, Paul stomping the wooden planks, middle-aged men and women on an adjoining roof . . . , boys and girls on nearby buildings, lying against the roof slopes and waving, the Beatles smiling and singing to each other in the wind."

The Fab Four were not only smiling and singing, they were doing so in a way that would later be described as "four musicians playing as no four ever would again." Derek Taylor, the Beatles' press agent, would have his own memories of the event. "I didn't go on the roof because I was busy with the press," he would recall. "Fielding the calls. The phones started to ring off the hook because everyone in London, in no time, knew the Beatles were performing on the roof, and it was fabulous. It was the first good, big, positive story without any snags for months and months. . . . By and large the calls were just from the press who were thrilled the boys were out playing music again."

Magnificent as it was, the concert lasted little more than forty minutes. Suddenly the police arrived, not only ordering the band to stop playing, but turning off the power to their electric instruments. Later, Ringo would express his feelings about the arrival of the law. "I always feel let down about the police," he would state. "Someone in the neighbourhood called the police, and when they came up I was playing away and I thought, 'Oh great! I hope they drag me off.' I *wanted* the cops to drag me off—'Get off those drums!'—because we were being filmed and it would have looked really great, kicking the cymbals and everything. Well, they didn't [drag us off], of course; they just came bumbling in: 'You've got to turn that sound down.' It could have been fabulous."

Although the rooftop performance did not end as dramatically as Ringo would have liked, it was a throwback to the glory days of the Fab Four's live performances. And it was something else; it was the last time that the Beatles would ever perform in public as a group.

It was also the only instance of real harmony that the band experienced while making *Let It Be*. During all that had led up to the rooftop performance, the rifts within the band had widened. John was making it increasingly clear that he wanted to spend more time with Yoko than with the band. George, who had been writing songs on his own, felt that they were being ignored by the others. Like John, he was convinced that Paul was trying to take over the group. George actually left the band for a short time and came back only when, as they had done previously with Ringo, the group coaxed him into returning.

By this time, even Paul had to admit that the group was moving hopelessly apart. Painfully,

AN ALARMING RUMOR

It was not surprising that a group of individuals as famous as the Beatles would be the subject of many rumors both individually and as a group. In the fall of 1969, one of the most widely spread rumors concerning the Fab Four emerged.

By September 1969, tensions within the band were mounting. Paul, in particular, was less publicly seen than at any time since the group had been formed. Then, on September 17, 1969, the Drake University student newspaper published an article titled "Is Paul McCartney Dead?" Other newspapers quickly picked up the story. Soon rumors began to spread about how the beloved Beatle had died.

One of the common stories stated that during a recording session in late 1966, Paul had a heated argument with his fellow Beatles. According to the story, he had driven off angrily in his car, crashed, and been killed in the one-car accident. To hide the tragic news from the public, the story continued, the Beatles had secretly replaced him with a young man who had won a Paul McCartney look-alike contest.

The startling story had arisen during a time when media reports on celebrities' activities and whereabouts were far less common, and many obsessive Beatles fans began looking for clues to prove that the rumor was true. Some claimed that by listening extremely carefully to the song "Strawberry Fields Forever" on the *Magical Mystery Tour* album, one could hear John stating, "I buried Paul." (Actually, John was saying "cranberry sauce.") Others believed that secret messages concerning Paul's death could be discovered by playing certain Beatles records backward.

The desire to find clues led some Beatles fans to believe that there was dire meaning in the fact that Paul was wearing a black rose in the *Magical Mystery Tour* film. Still others were convinced that Paul's appearance with his back to the camera on the *Sgt. Pepper* album cover was clear indication that he had died.

The most widely discussed clues were those that supposedly could be found on the *Abbey Road* album, which, although recorded after the *Let It Be* album, was actually released before *Let It Be*. Those who believed the "Paul is dead" rumor interpreted the album's cover as showing the Beatles in a funeral procession rather than walking across the street to their recording studio. To those who believed this "clue," John, dressed in all white, was the preacher; Ringo, clad in all black, was the mourner; George, wearing denim pants and shirt, was the gravedigger; and Paul, barefoot and out of step, was the corpse.

The dramatic cover photograph of the four Beatles crossing Abbey Road also showed a car parked on the

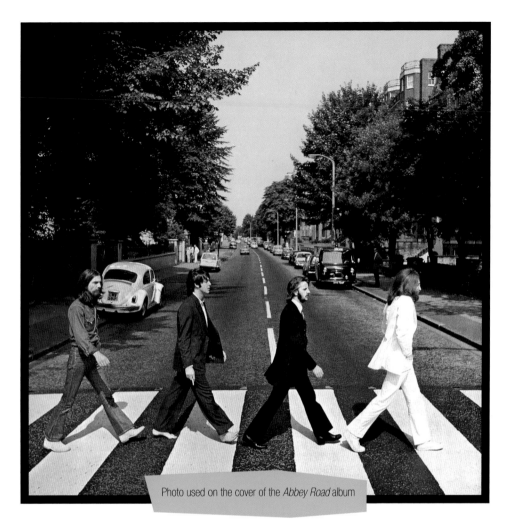

Photo used on the cover of the *Abbey Road* album

road. Its license plate read "28IF." Many of those who believed the "Paul is dead" rumor were also certain that the positioning of the car and the license had been deliberate and that 28IF meant that Paul would have been 28 years old *if* he had lived.

Far-fetched as the rumors were, they became widespread in America. "Paul is dead" articles and songs dedicated to his memory continued to be written even after November 1969, when *Life* magazine published an interview with Paul complete with a recently taken photograph of him on the cover.

As John would comment, "Paul McCartney couldn't die without the world knowing it. It's impossible— he can't go on holiday without the world knowing it. It's just insanity—but it's a great plug for *Abbey Road*." He was right on both counts. Paul was indeed very much alive, and thanks partially to the enormous publicity the *Abbey Road* album gained from the supposed clue on its cover, it realized even greater sales success than *Sgt. Pepper's Lonely Hearts Club Band*.

he was forced to recognize that rather than becoming a film showing the Beatles writing, rehearsing, and making an album, *Let It Be* was turning into a revelation of the Beatles on the verge of splitting apart. "I'd talked them into *Let It Be,*" Paul would later state. "Then we had terrible arguments—so we'd get the breakup of the Beatles on film instead of what we really wanted. It was probably a better story—a sad story, but there you are." The most fabled musical group of all time had reached a point from which there seemed no turning back. John would express it simply. "We couldn't play the game anymore," he would explain. "We couldn't do it anymore."

As if all that was going on within the group was not difficult enough, there was another issue that would contribute to their breakup. Their business and financial situation was far from what it should have been. As a manager, Brian Epstein had been brilliant in promoting the Beatles. He had made their groundbreaking first *Ed Sullivan Show* appearance possible. He had gotten them their first recording contract. He had capitalized on their early success by arranging tours and appearances that made the Beatles a household name throughout the world. But as a financial manager, he had fallen far short. Part of it was due to the enormous amount of time he was forced to spend just promoting the Beatles; dealing with the thousands of requests for their time; and arranging their tours, moviemaking, and other nonstop activities. Even more was due to the fact that he was simply unable to keep track or control of the overwhelming amount of Beatles merchandise that was being sold throughout the world. Probably no one could have, especially in those pre-computer days. But the result was that companies, large and small, were selling tens of millions of dollars' worth of products with the Beatles' name or images on them without paying the Fab Four the percentage of the sales they were due. As John would state, "Brian Epstein was a beautiful guy: he was an intuitive theatrical guy and he knew we had something and he presented us well. But he had lousy business advice. He was taken advantage of—we all were."

To try to correct the situation after Epstein's death, the Beatles formed their own company, called Apple Corporation. It included a record label that would allow the group to release all of their own future records along with those of promising new musical performers. With no one person really in charge of running it, however, the company soon ran into financial difficulty. "People," John recalled, "were robbing us and living on us to the tune of eighteen or twenty thousand pounds a week that was rolling out of Apple and nobody was doing anything about it."

There was no question about it. The Beatles needed a new manager to set their finances straight. It was the one thing upon which they all agreed. But deciding upon just who that person should be would lead to further disputes within the group. Paul insisted that his businessman father-in-law be hired for the job. But the others felt that Allen Klein, the man who had managed the Rolling Stones to riches, was a better choice. When Klein was selected after several bitter arguments, even Paul, who had tried so hard to keep the group together, knew that his days as a Beatle were coming to an end.

John, George, and Ringo, each for his reasons, also knew that the end was at hand. But the breakup of the Beatles would not take place without one final magnificent gasp. In April 1969, the band came together to produce what would be their final album, *Abbey Road*. And, despite

A moment of unity during the recording of *Let It Be*

the turmoil and tension they had been experiencing, they were determined to make one last great musical statement.

Rather than produce the record themselves on their own Apple label, they went back to EMI's recording studios and persuaded George Martin to guide the album through its production. The group, Paul told Martin, wanted to create a final album "the way we used to do it." Martin's response was direct. "If the album's going to be the way it used to be," he replied, "then all of you have got to be the way you used to be."

For one last time, they came together again, and *Abbey Road* was their crowning achievement. It contained a song written by George, titled "Something," a song that John would call his favorite on the entire album, one that famed pop singer Frank Sinatra would regard as the greatest love song ever written. Also released as a single, "Something" would become the first Beatles number-one single that was not a Lennon-McCartney composition. The album also featured another song by George, titled "Here Comes the Sun." Although not released as a single, it continues to rank among those songs played most frequently on the radio. *Abbey Road* also featured a children's song titled "Octopus Garden," written by Ringo, and the album included the only drum solo ever to appear on a Beatles recording.

As they created their final album, the Beatles could not help but be influenced by the feelings they were experiencing as they were splitting apart. Deciding that he had to change his scenery for at least one day, George went to visit his musician friend Eric Clapton at his country home. Borrowing one of Clapton's guitars, George took a stroll through one of his friend's gardens, where he began writing "Here Comes the Sun," one of *Abbey Road*'s most memorable songs. It was, George would later state, such a great release just being by himself in the sun that the song just came to him.

Ironically, the next-to-last song on *Abbey Road* was titled "The End," followed by fourteen seconds of silence. And indeed, the end had come. Before the year 1970 was over, the Beatles had irrevocably split apart. Despite the hopes and pleading of fans, there was no going back. The split had been too long in the making. "It was like the wind-down to a divorce," Ringo would reflect. "A divorce usually doesn't just happen suddenly. There are months and years . . . until you finally say 'Oh, let's end it.'" George Martin, who had been as close an observer of the group as anyone, had long felt that the breakup was inevitable.

Daily Mirror newspaper headline announcing Paul quitting the band

"They'd always been having to consider the group," he would state, "so they were a prisoner of that—and I think they eventually got fed up with it. They wanted to live life like other people."

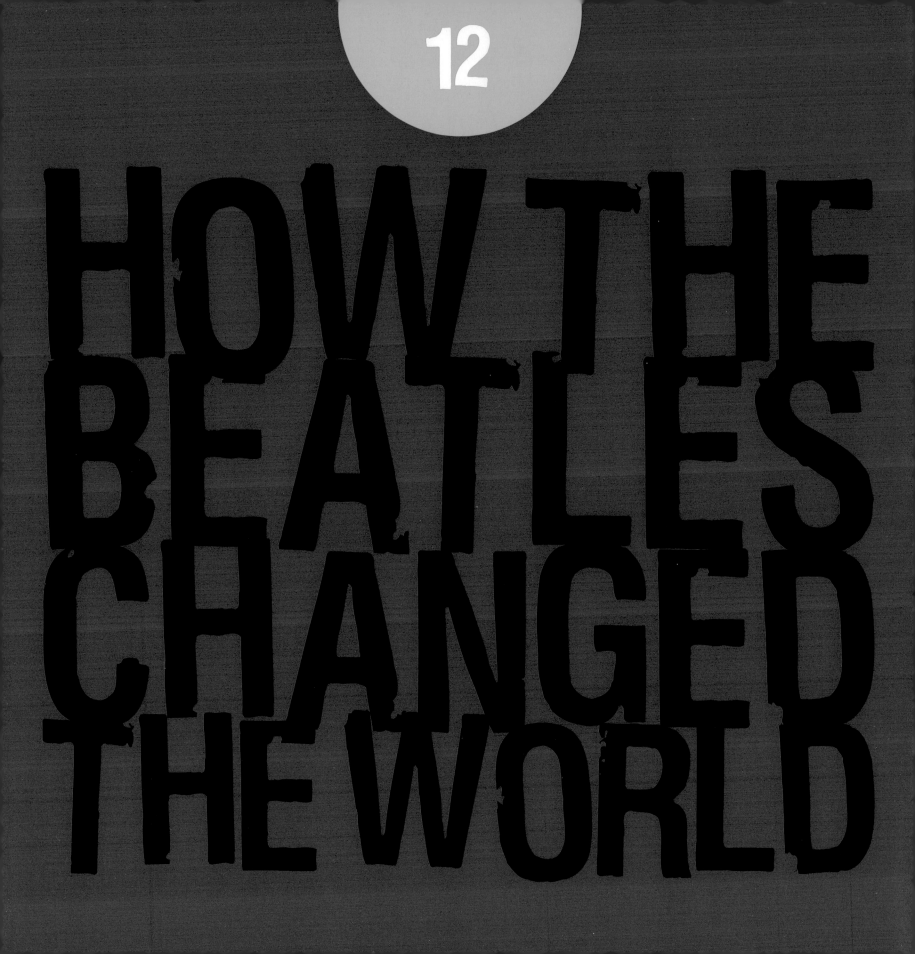

HOW THE BEATLES CHANGED THE WORLD

PEACE. **PEACE.**

By the time their days as a group were over, the Beatles had

established themselves as among the most brilliant songwriters and innovative musicians the world had ever known. But to assess their contributions only on their musical accomplishments or their movie triumphs or the ways in which they influenced fashion would be an enormous mistake, for they did much, much more. Put simply, the Beatles changed the world.

The Fab Four had an impact on tens of millions of people throughout the world in ways that musicians had never had before. They did nothing less than change popular culture forever. They became the catalysts and symbols of the social and cultural revolutions of the 1960s. In the process, as author Jim Wentzel has observed, "They changed the world's attitude toward what the younger generation could accomplish."

As the most popular musical group in the world, adored by millions of young people, the Beatles could not have avoided having a gigantic influence on them. They could have, as other pop music groups did, written angry, even rebellious songs. Instead, they chose to convey very different kinds of messages to a generation of young people searching for meaning in a tumultuous and often confusing world. Their messages were of hope and love and peace and imagination. And their meaning was unmistakably clear: "All You Need Is Love," "Give Peace a Chance," "Say the Word and You Shall Be Free." The Beatles would continue to deliver these messages until their days together were over. It was not by accident that in their final album,

The Berlin Wall was the ultimate symbol of the Cold War.

Abbey Road, produced as the 1960s were coming to a close, they would ask everyone, for one last time, to "Come Together."

The Beatles burst upon the scene during an extraordinary period in history. The 1960s was a time of extreme tension and unrest. It was an era in which the Communist world, led by the Soviet Union, stood toe-to-toe with the free world in the Cold War, a dangerous clash of ideologies that ultimately led to the wildly unpopular Vietnam War. The Cuban Missile Crisis made nuclear confrontation a very real possibility. Tragic events such as the assassination of America's popular president John F. Kennedy; his brother, Robert; and inspirational African American leader Dr. Martin Luther King, Jr., added to a widespread feeling of uncertainty and fear about the future.

Among those who felt most uncertain of all were the tens of millions of those who dwelled in countries that had come under the control of Communism. Living behind what was termed the Iron Curtain, they had no freedom or hope of ever being free. It was the impact that the Beatles would have on these people, and particularly the millions of young people among them, that would lead to the greatest and most astounding Beatles contribution of all.

It was perhaps best expressed by author Bob Spitz, who wrote, "The Beatles made [an] impact on human history, because their influence [was] liberating for generations of nowhere men living in misery beyond the Iron Curtain. Something in their songs . . . appealed to everybody who wanted to become free as a bird. . . . Their songs . . . helped many freedom-loving people to come together for revolutions in Prague and Warsaw, Beijing and Bucharest, Berlin and Moscow. The Beatles [have] been an inspiration for those who take the long and winding road to freedom."

Nowhere did these extraordinary developments take place in a more amazing manner than in the Soviet Union itself. "It sounds ridiculous," famed movie director Milos Forman has stated, "but I'm convinced the Beatles are partly responsible for the fall of Communism." Dr. Yury Pelyushonok, who grew up in Russia, agrees. "The Beatles," he has written, "had this tremendous impact on Soviet kids. The Soviet authorities thought of the Beatles as a secret Cold War weapon. The kids lost their interest in all Soviet unshakable dogmas and ideals, and stopped thinking of an English-speaking person as the enemy." Russian leaders, in fact, regarded all rock-and-roll groups as not only decadent but also a real threat to Communism. They hated electric guitars, which, to them, were the very symbols of this threat. Most of all, they hated the Beatles.

Throughout Russia and all the countries under Soviet control, the playing of Beatles music was forbidden, and all Beatles records were banned. It went without saying that the Fab Four would never be allowed to perform behind the Iron Curtain. Recalling his youth, one Russian citizen remembered that "I was scared if I said anything good about the Beatles, I would be arrested." He had good reason to be frightened. Throughout the Soviet Union, young people had indeed been arrested for attempting to smuggle in Beatles records. Students had been expelled from Russian universities for owning a Beatles album.

An article in one of Russia's leading state-run newspapers told the story of two teenagers who had tried to cross the border into Poland so that they could make their way to Germany, where, they had heard, a Beatles concert was to be held. The two young people had been discovered hiding under a railway car during a border check. And they had a forbidden guitar with them. The article's headline stated, "Today they're playing the Beatles. Tomorrow..." The headline ended there. But its message was clear. It was only one small step from playing Beatles music to corruption, even rebellion.

It may have been rebellion, but throughout Russia, teenagers were determined to listen to Beatles music. They were so determined that they took enormous risks. Tape recorders were increasingly appearing in Russia. Young people began listening to Radio Luxembourg, one of the only foreign radio stations not jammed by Soviet authorities. They then tape-recorded whatever Beatles songs the station played. Although few citizens were allowed to travel outside Russia, a few of them who did smuggled in Beatles records and albums, which were also then tape-recorded.

Antoine, Radio Luxembourg presenter

In the most risky and ingenious procedure of all, Russian young people who had no tape recorders actually made their own recordings out of whatever Beatles music they could obtain. Records in those days were made of vinyl. But Russian authorities kept the sale of vinyl strictly regulated. That did not stop determined Soviet teens. Discovering that medical X-ray film was a passable substitute, they cut X-ray film into the shape of a record, carved grooves in it, and made Beatles recordings. It was not a perfect substitute for vinyl, but it worked. When held up to the light, the background of an X-ray recording often disclosed bones and joints that had appeared on the original X-ray. It was not long before the

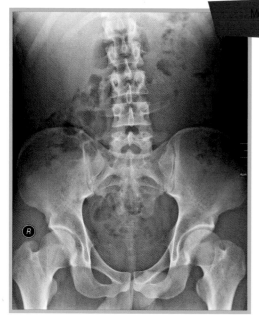

X-ray Beatles recordings were being referred to as Rock 'n' Roll on Bones.

It was not only young people who became involved in the innovative recordings. Adults, sensing a lucrative underground business opportunity, began obtaining as many of these homemade Beatles records as they could and secretly selling them throughout the Soviet Union. They and those who bought the records were taking an enormous risk. The penalties for either buying or selling the forbidden recordings included substantial fines and even imprisonment.

In finding a way to hear Beatles records, Russian youngsters had proven themselves ingenious. But they wanted to do more than just listen to the Fab Four. They wanted to play their music themselves. And that meant gaining possession of something as illicit as a Beatles recording—an electric guitar. The Soviet government had declared the electric guitar to be an evil instrument and an enemy of the Soviet people. There were no electric guitars for sale in any store throughout Russia.

Russian teenagers had only a vague notion of what an electric guitar was. But with the same ingenuity and determination they had displayed in making X-ray records, they doggedly learned the secrets of how one could be made. One of the best ways to get started, they determined, was to do everything they could to get hold of Beatles photographs and study what their guitars looked like. Those teens fortunate enough to be able to attend an occasional exhibition of musical instruments from Soviet East Germany spent hours looking at and drawing sketches of the electric guitars on display.

Armed with this information, young people started to create the body of an electric guitar out of whatever

A pronounced "enemy" of the Soviet people

appropriately sized pieces of wood they could find. Once that was done, they needed to find strings for their homemade instrument. At first it seemed like that would be a real problem, but then they discovered that the type of wire that the military used for many purposes was suitable for guitar strings and was readily available.

A much greater challenge was getting their hands on an essential part of an electric guitar known as a pickup. It is a device that captures the mechanical vibrations from the guitar and gives it its distinctive sound. That problem was solved when the popular Russian magazine *Young Technician* published an article explaining that a pickup was very much like a telephone receiver. The response from guitar-making teens throughout Russia was both immediate and spectacular. As Yury Pelyushonok has written, "As if on command, all of the magnetic coils disappeared from the receivers hanging in telephone booths across the whole Soviet Union. In just one day, the entire pay-phone network was disabled in all of the cities and villages."

Russian teens stole telephone receivers to make the pickup and pickguard for electric guitars, shown here.

Pelyushonok has clear memories of how he and a friend, like thousands of other Russian young people, went on a search to pilfer the telephone receivers they needed for their guitars. "By the time [we] had gathered the courage to 'do the deed,'" he wrote, "there wasn't a single telephone receiver left intact in the entire city. To make a pickup for a six-string guitar we needed at least three receivers. We went from pay phone to pay phone, but all we could find where the mouthpiece was supposed to be were big, gaping holes. Growing weary of our search, we decided to approach the problem from another angle. Instead of prowling the city, we waited in ambush on our own street for the telephone repairmen to show up. To speed things along, we placed numerous calls to the telephone company, complaining in indignant adult voices, 'It's disgraceful! When are they finally going to repair

RUSSIAN RUMORS

As in the West, Russian teens' obsession with all things pertaining to the Beatles led to widespread rumors concerning the Fab Four. Rumors continually appeared stating that one of the Beatles had died. And, as in Britain and America, when the "Paul is dead" rumor surfaced, the belief arose that if one played a Beatles record backward, clues to which Beatle had died would be revealed. In Russia, however, that was not a practical solution. Since no one owned a store-bought record, that particular rumor quickly disappeared.

Other supposedly true stories, however, persisted. One of them grew out of young Russian Beatles fans' concern that John, the original Beatle, had been working so long and so hard that he was bound to lose his voice. That led to a related rumor. According to that one, John would never lose his voice because he always drank a dozen raw eggs before recording a song.

Another rumor stated that for safety purposes, the Beatles gave their live concerts while encased in steel cages. Another one claimed that, for their safety, the Fab Four drove around in armored cars, flew only in military aircraft, and landed only in secret military airfields.

The Rolls-Royce formerly owned by John Lennon

One of the most common rumors of all involved no less a personage than England's Queen Elizabeth. According to this tale, the Queen was so impressed with John in particular that she had given him one of the most valuable cars ever made. Some of the rumor-spreaders said that it was made entirely of silver. Others stated that it was constructed of pure gold. Whichever version of the story those young Russians believed, they took it as another sign of just how important their heroes were.

The most popular and most accepted Beatles rumor of all stated that although they were strictly prohibited from performing in the Soviet Union, John, Paul, George, and Ringo had actually given an impromptu concert in Russia when their airplane stopped to refuel on the band's way to Japan. Because they were not allowed on Soviet soil, the rumor held, the Beatles gave their concert on one of the aircraft's wings. It is a rumor that actually persists today, kept alive by individuals who swear that the secret concert took place in their community and that they were there to hear it.

the telephones in our area!!! We're sick and tired of waiting!' The repair crew showed up fairly quickly, but literally minutes after they'd fixed all the phones in the entire area, there wasn't a single working receiver to be found intact."

The final component the young people needed to make their own guitars was an amplifier to magnify the sound of their instrument. Like the receivers housed in the telephone booths, they found what they needed in loudspeakers that were lodged on tall poles. Such speakers, Pelyushonok wrote, "were hung along the streets during special holidays. On these occasions, when the Soviet government would stage official events, the sound of deafening marches and congratulatory speeches would boom from every pole in the city. These 25-50 watt holiday speakers were a real godsend to those of us who [were making] electric guitars. The speakers would vanish from the poles during the night, right under the noses of the watchful police."

Explaining why he and so many Russian teenagers engaged in such outright pilfering, Pelyushonok wrote, "It's not as if we were a horde of barbarians destroying everything in our path. [We'd] sooner starve than steal a piece of bread. But when it came to our dream, we'd do anything just to keep up with the Beatles."

In Russia, as in other countries throughout the world, keeping up with the Beatles meant dressing like them as well as listening to and playing their music. Although it was nearly impos-sible to find velvet clothing in the Soviet Union, stores sold bolts of velvet for draperies and for covering sofas and chairs. In many Russian communities, girls made velvet jackets close to those that the Beatles wore, for their boyfriends. Beatle boots, Ringo bracelets, and Lennon eyeglasses came into great demand.

Much to the consternation of both Soviet and political leaders and school officials, boys increasingly

The Beatles' style in the late 1960s inspired a secret fashion revolution among Soviet teens.

Many years after the fall of the Soviet Union, Paul McCartney now performs in Russia.

started wearing their hair long, just like the Beatles did. Knowing that the hairstyle would never be accepted by school authorities, boys, before setting off to school, combed their long hair from their necks and pinned it up with hidden hairpins. Some smeared oil into their hair so that their Beatles hairdos would be hidden behind their ears.

The Beatles, Russian musical producer Stas Namin proclaimed, "influenced everything—

our music, our way of dressing, our way of living, everything." "No sooner had a school boy had his first taste of the Beatles than he became smitten with John or Paul or George or Ringo," Yury Pelyushonok wrote. "And depending on just how badly smitten they were, the kids would either pick up a guitar or sit down behind a set of drums. Once they heard the Beatles, everyone over here began imitating them and forming four-man bands. . . ."

"Something strange was going on," Pelyushonok would add, " if Beatle songs could be heard from every apartment that had a teenager with a tape recorder living in it . . . and the word Beatles came up at least once in every hundred words spoken by the average Russian school child. In the West, this situation was officially named Beatlemania. In the Soviet Union, they preferred to keep an official silence on the matter."

It was more than Beatlemania. Before the Beatles, generations of Russian students steadfastly resisted learning English. Today, thousands of Russian adults who were teenagers in the 1960s, including Russia's Deputy Prime Minister Sergei Ivanov, attest to the fact that while they paid no attention to the English that was being taught in the schools, they enthusiastically learned the language from hours and hours of listening to Beatles songs. More important, it was from the Beatles' songs, listened to over and over again, that two generations of young Russians living in an oppressed society received messages of love and peace and hope and freedom.

The Beatles, Stas Namin proclaimed, "produced a cultural revolution, the cultural revolution that destroyed the Soviet Union." Speaking of how Russian youngsters rejected the freedom-inhibiting tenets of communism thanks to what they learned from the Beatles, Russia's leading rock music writer, Art Troitsky, wrote, "In the . . . West they had whole institutions which spent tens of millions of dollars for undermining the Soviet system, and I'm sure that the impact of all those stupid Cold War institutions has been much smaller than the impact of the Beatles." It has all been confirmed by none other than General Secretary of the Communist Party, Mikhail Gorbachev, who, from 1985 until the collapse of Soviet Communism in 1991, served as the last head of state of the Soviet Union. "More than any ideology, more than any religion, more than Vietnam or any war or nuclear bomb," Gorbachev proclaimed, "the single most important reason for the diffusion of the Cold War was . . . the Beatles."

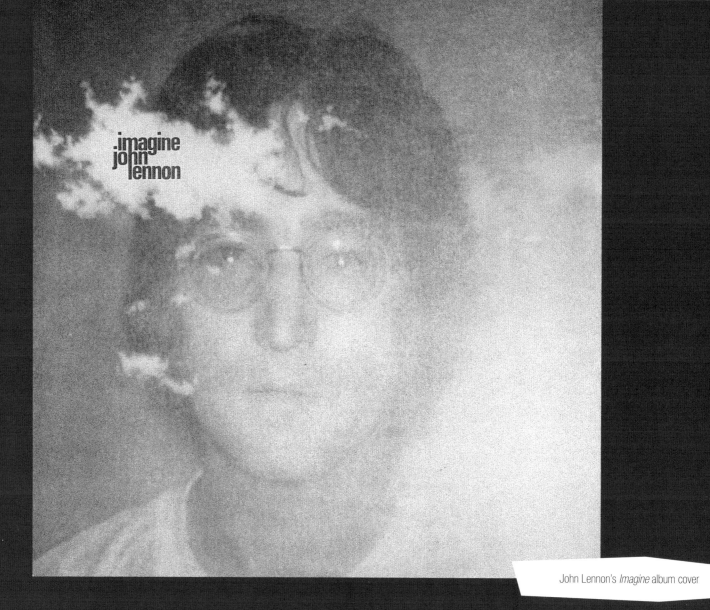

imagine
john
lennon

John Lennon's *Imagine* album cover

Although the breakup of the Beatles was a gradual process, the official end of the most popular and influential music group in history did not take place until April 1970, when Paul announced publicly that he was leaving the group. Although each of them had already gone their separate ways, John, George, and Ringo did not publicly confirm the breakup until eight months later.

Of all the Beatles, it had been John who, for the longest time, had wanted to go out on his own and pursue his own new career. As far as the Fab Four's movie director Richard Lester was concerned, John could have become a major movie star. After watching John's critically acclaimed performance in *How I Won the War*, Lester stated, "I told him then he could do anything he wanted in films. But he wasn't interested. It came too easily to him."

What John really wanted to do was to write songs and make albums on his own. Most of all, he wanted to create songs of inspiration and hope that were even stronger than those he had written as a Beatle. The first album he made was titled *John Lennon/Plastic Ono Band*. Then he made what is considered by many to be the greatest of all his musical contributions. *Imagine* is still regarded as one of the finest albums ever produced. Its title song became and remains the anthem for all those who share John's desire for peace and world harmony.

In the 1970s, John settled permanently in New York City, where he made ten other albums. He also wrote and recorded a single titled "Whatever Gets You Through the Night," which rose to number one on the charts. Through it all, he remained one of the world's most recognizable advocates for peace. He even turned his wedding to Yoko Ono into a message for peace.

After their marriage ceremony on March 20, 1969, John and Yoko took advantage of the extraordinary attention their wedding had received by inviting reporters from around the world into their hotel honeymoon suite. There, for seven days and nights, they staged what they called Bed-Ins for Peace by remaining in bed and talking continually to the hordes of journalists about the benefits of world harmony.

In the mid-1970s, after the birth of his son Sean, John made a dramatic life change. He took a five-year break from the music industry and devoted himself full-time to being a househusband and father. By 1980 he was ready to resume his songwriting and recording career, and in the fall of that year, he and Yoko made an album together titled *Double Fantasy*.

Fans at a vigil for John Lennon after his murder

But then tragedy struck. On December 8, 1980, while walking back to their home from a recording studio, John was shot and killed by a deranged fan. It was not only tragic but ironic. At the age of forty, the man who had been one of the world's most influential advocates of peace and love had been struck down by violence.

The grief that followed John's murder

was both enormous and extraordinary. As author Phillip Norman wrote, "The scale of grief after John's murder was—and remains—something unique in modern times. Unlike the mourning for John F. Kennedy seventeen years earlier, it was not confined largely to the victim's own homeland. . . . It was an utterly spontaneous outpouring of misery far across continents by those who felt they had lost an intimate, inspirational friend."

Among the thousands of tributes to John following his death was a song by George Harrison titled "All Those Years Ago," which included the lyrics "I always looked up to you." Like John, George had launched his post-Beatle career with a solo album, titled *All Things Must Pass.* Not surprisingly, it contained songs reflective of George's continual spiritual exploration and his ongoing quest for life's meaning. Among its songs was "My Sweet Lord," which went on to become a number-one single in the United States, Great Britain, and several other countries.

George's songwriting blossomed after the Beatles' breakup.

As George continued to write songs that were not only captivating in their melodies but often profound in their lyrics, it became clear that while a Beatle, his songwriting abilities were never adequately appreciated. As George Martin would state, "George . . . was never treated . . . as having the same quality of songwriting, by anyone—by John, by Paul, or by me. I'm as guilty in that respect. I was the guy who used to say: 'If he's got a song, we'll let him have it on the album'—very condescendingly. I know he must have felt really bad about that. Gradually he kept persevering, and his songs did get better—until eventually they got extremely good. 'Something' is a wonderful song—but we didn't give him credit for it, and we never really thought, 'He's going to be a great songwriter.'

"The other problem was that he didn't have a collaborator. John always had Paul to bounce ideas off. Even if he didn't actually write the song with Paul, he was a kind of competitive mate. George was a loner, and I'm afraid that was made worse by the three of us. I'm sorry about that now."

Interestingly, it was Ringo who recognized George's songwriting talents more than any of the others, particularly during the Beatles' last days together. "George," he would state, "was blossoming as a songwriter with 'Something' and 'While My Guitar Gently Weeps'—are you kidding me? Two of the finest love songs ever written, and they're really on a par with what John and Paul or anyone else of that time wrote. They're beautiful songs. It's interesting that George was coming to the fore and we were breaking up."

In 1971, a year after the release of *All Things Must Pass*, George made an enormous humanitarian contribution. Aware that the people of Bangladesh were suffering terribly from both famine and disease, he organized a concert designed to raise money for their relief. The first-ever concert of its kind, it featured performances by George, Bob Dylan, Eric Clapton, Billy Preston, and Ravi Shankar. A highlight was the appearance of Ringo, the first time two ex-Beatles had been reunited onstage since the band's breakup. Titled *The Concert for Bangladesh*, the charitable event was an enormous success and was eventually made into both an album and a film.

In the early 1980s, George's solo career took a most unexpected turn. He

A scene from *Monty Python's Life of Brian*, a movie which George financed.

was friendly with Michael Palin who, along with Eric Idle and John Cleese, had won fame by creating the highly successful British television comedy series *Monty Python's Flying Circus*. The group had begun making a movie titled *Life of Brian*, but midway through the filming they had run out of financing. George, who had been a huge fan of the Monty Python series, came to the rescue by contributing the £4 million needed to complete the movie. *Life of Brian* turned out to be a colossal box-office hit. And it brought George into the movie business as a partner in a newly formed moviemaking company called HandMade. The company would go on to make more than twenty successful films, including *Time Bandits*, which is today regarded by many as a classic.

Throughout the 1980s, George also continued recording and again produced a number-one single with "Got My Mind Set on You." He then teamed up with fellow artists Roy Orbison, Bob Dylan, Tom Petty, and Jeff Lynne and created a supergroup called The Traveling Wilburys. Among the albums they created was *Traveling Wilburys Vol. 1,* which won the Grammy Award for Best Performance by a Duo or Group in 1989.

By this time, George, as had John a decade earlier, decided to remove himself from the public eye. Aside from his desire to be with his second wife, Olivia, and his son, there was another reason for his wishing to be out of the limelight. From the moment he heard of John's murder, he had become seriously concerned that the same thing could happen to him. He had installed the most sophisticated security systems available at his estate called Friar Park. To make certain that he was personally guarded by those he could trust, he had made his brother his security chief.

But these measures failed to prevent his worst fears from happening. At three o'clock in the morning on December 30, 1999, George was awakened by the sound of breaking glass. Racing downstairs to the first floor, he came face-to-face with a knife-wielding man. After trying in vain to reason with the intruder, George tackled him. In the process he was stabbed in the chest. "I felt my chest deflate and the flow of blood to my mouth. I truly thought I was dying," George later said. Fortunately, his cries of pain and alarm attracted Olivia, who rushed to the scene, picked up a heavy brass lamp, and struck the attacker across the head, rendering him unconscious. George was then rushed to a hospital with a collapsed lung, but thanks to Olivia's heroic actions, his life had been spared.

George had narrowly escaped the same violent fate that had befallen John. But he could not escape the dreaded disease lung cancer. On November 29, 2001, after a valiant battle against the illness, he passed away at the age of fifty-eight. The tributes to the man known as the "quiet Beatle" rivaled those that John's murder had elicited. On the first anniversary of George's death, his close friend Eric Clapton headlined a memorial concert for him at London's Royal Hall. Aside from honoring a fallen Beatle, it became a much-heralded reunion of sorts with both Paul and Ringo taking part in the tribute.

George had been known as the quiet Beatle. And his songwriting talents were indeed unappreciated for far too long. But he had never lost sight of the extraordinary changes the Beatles had brought to the world. Assessing what he thought were the Beatles' greatest accomplishments, he stated, "I think we gave hope to the Beatle fans. We gave them a positive feeling that there was a sunny day ahead and that there was a good time to be had and that you are your own person and that the government doesn't own you. There were those kinds of messages in a lot of our songs."

Paul, whose songwriting talents had never been unappreciated, began his post-Beatle career with what would become one of his most popular hits. He had actually written "Maybe I'm Amazed" in 1969 just before the Fab Four's breakup and had dedicated the song to his wife, Linda, whom he credited with having helped him get through the trauma of the band's splitting apart. Released in April 1970, as a

Fan memorial for George Harrison near Abbey Road

part of Paul's album titled *McCartney,* "Maybe I'm Amazed" became a favorite of disc jockeys throughout the world, who filled the airways with the song. In 1974, after forming the band Wings, he produced an album titled *Band on the Run,* which included two hit songs, one titled "Jet," the other with the same name as the album. *Band on the Run* would gain the distinction of having sold more than five million copies, making it the most successful album of any of those produced by a former Beatle. A year before the release of *Band on the Run,* Paul had written and sung the title song of a James Bond movie, "Live and Let Die," one of the most acclaimed movie theme songs ever composed and performed. On December 16, 1976, in recognition of all that he had achieved and was still accomplishing, England's Queen Elizabeth II presented him with a title of nobility. The man who had been called the "cute Beatle" was now *Sir* Paul McCartney.

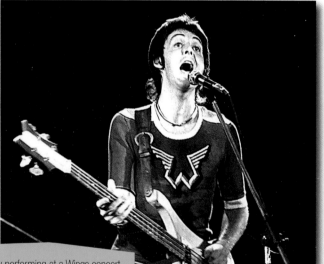
Paul McCartney performing at a Wings concert

Throughout the rest of the 1970s and into the 1980s and 1990s, Paul continued to make albums and to tour, mainly with Wings. In 1981 and 1982, he collaborated on two songs with Michael Jackson: "Say, Say, Say," which became part of Jackson's *Pipes of Peace* album, and "The Girl Is Mine," which was included in Jackson's megahit album *Thriller.* Also in 1982, "Ebony and Ivory," a song Paul wrote with Stevie Wonder, was released and reached number one on both the American and British charts.

For Paul, the new millennium has been a period of continued acclaim and commercial success. In 2002 his status as the most valued entertainer in the world was confirmed when he was offered four million dollars to perform in Las Vegas for just one night. In 2003 and 2004 he took Russia by storm, first with his Back in the USSR concert and then with his show staged next to the czar's winter place in St. Petersburg, where the Communist revolution had taken place.

Throughout the 2000s Paul has continued to produce critically acclaimed albums, including *Chaos and Creation in the Backyard* (2005), in which he played nearly all the instruments; *Memory Almost Full* (2007), which to date has sold some two million copies worldwide; and *Kisses on the Bottom* (2012), in which he paid tribute to outstanding pop-music songs written by composers other than the Beatles. In 2011, Paul displayed his versatility and love of all music by creating the score for a classical ballet titled *Ocean's Kingdom,* which was commissioned by the New York City Ballet.

Today, Paul is the most recognizable and sought-after entertainer in the world. In October 2001, he organized and performed at the Concert for New York, a benefit event honoring those members of the New York City Fire and Police Departments who had responded to the 9/11 tragedy, those who lost their lives in the catastrophe, and those who continued to work in the rescue and recovery efforts. In December 2010, Paul received a prestigious Kennedy Center Honor. In June 2012, he was the featured performer at the Queen's Diamond Jubilee concert. And it was no accident that those who organized and staged the 2012 Olympic Games in London selected Sir Paul McCartney to perform the finale of the games' opening ceremonies.

Now more than seventy years old, Paul is revered by a whole new generation of music fans. He gains great satisfaction every time he realizes that the songs he wrote as a Beatle have as much meaning for today's young people as they did for their parents and grandparents. "I do these songs still," he says. 'Let It Be' and the like. And to actually see young kids crying over the spirit in the song, I'm very proud of that."

Ringo, the other surviving member of the Beatles, has also enjoyed considerable success in his post-Fab Four days. Performing solo has, in fact, allowed him to gain the spotlight that was not possible for him to attain as a Beatle. During his Beatle days, Ringo was given very few songs to sing by himself. And even though John once declared, "Ringo was the greatest rock and roll drummer I ever saw," the nature of the Beatles' performances allowed no room for drum solos.

As Paul would later state, "I think Ringo was always paranoid that he wasn't a great drummer because he never used to solo. . . . Until *Abbey Road,* there was never a drum solo in the Beatles'

Paul McCartney with Michael Jackson

act, and consequently other drummers would say that although they liked his style, Ringo wasn't *technically* a very good drummer. It was a bit condescending and I think we let it go too far. I think his feel and soul and the way he was rock solid with his tempo was a great attribute."

Along with having achieved two number-one hits, "Photograph" and "You're Sixteen," Ringo has remained in the public eye through the several television programs he has hosted and the many TV commercials he has made. He became a favorite of toddlers and pre-schoolers by playing the role of Mr. Conductor during the first season of the highly popular children's television series *Shining Time Station.* An accomplished actor, he has appeared in feature roles in several movies, including *The Magic Christian, Blindman,* and *Caveman.* And he has acquired a whole new generation of fans through the continual concert tours he has undertaken with his Ringo Starr and His All-Starr Band.

Despite the tensions that played a major role in the Beatles' breakup, Ringo, perhaps more than any of the others, always had a special affection for his fellow band members. His heartfelt musical tribute to George during the concert commemorating the first anniversary of his death led one reviewer to state, "Ringo Starr caught everyone with a tear in their eye with a rendition of 'Photograph,' a composition he wrote with George, which seemed to sum up how everyone felt." On another occasion, when asked to sum up his feelings about the Beatles, Ringo, always the most emotional of the group, stated, "They became the closest friends I'd ever had. I was an only

Ringo Starr playing with his All-Starr Band

child and suddenly I felt as though I'd got three brothers. We really looked out for each other and we had many laughs together. . . . There were always pressures. Someone always wanted something: an interview, a hello, an autograph, to be seen with us, to speak to my dog, what-ever. So the four of us were really close. I loved it. I loved those guys. We took care of each other and we were the only ones who had that experience of being Beatles. No one else knows what that's like."

Ringo was right. Only he and John and Paul and George know what it really meant to be one of the Fab Four. What much of the world still knows, how-ever, is that the Beatles have never lost their appeal.

During a 1963 interview, when asked how long he thought people would remain interested in the Beatles, Paul replied, "We just hope we're gonna have quite a run." No one, including Paul, could have imagined how long a run it would be. Almost forty-five years after the group's breakup, nearly thirty-five years after John's tragic death, and almost fifteen years after George's passing, the Beatles still command worldwide attention.

Ringo found new fame with young children as Mr. Conductor on *Shining Time Station*.

Beatles tribute bands, featuring impersonators of the Fab Four playing Beatles songs, abound on both sides of the Atlantic. The famous Cirque du Soleil continues to stage an elaborate the-atrical production titled *LOVE,* featuring Beatles music.

At the height of the band's popularity, a British professor observed that, "You can walk down any street of the most primitive village in a country where no one speaks English and hear children chanting the words of [a] Beatles hit." It is still true today. The soundtrack album to the 2001 movie *I Am Sam* comprised entirely of Beatles songs, sung by modern pop artists, has been a huge success. Most significantly, the Beatles' *Anthology 1* has been the bestselling album of the 2000s and, as *Rolling Stone* has stated, "Kids still go mental the first time they hear 'Eight Days a Week.'"

THE FIFTH BEATLE

Throughout the storied career of the Beatles, there were individuals who had such a strong association with the Fab Four that, both in the press and the entertainment industry, they have been called Fifth Beatles. They include such early performers with the group as Stu Sutcliffe, the bass player of the five-member Beatles group that played in Hamburg, and Pete Best, who was the band's drummer in Hamburg until he was replaced by Ringo.

The two non-band members most frequently referred to as the Fifth Beatle are Brian Epstein and George Martin. Epstein's involvement as the group's manager is commonly regarded as having been essential in the Beatles' rise to international fame. John, in particular, was convinced that Epstein's sudden death in 1967 was the beginning of the Beatles' breakup.

Important as Epstein was to the group, there are many who believe that George Martin was even more entitled to be called the Fifth Beatle. Martin brilliantly produced most of the Beatles' records and continually encouraged them to be as innovative as they could. He also contributed his own musical talents to the group, such as by playing the piano on several recordings.

Two other Fifth Beatles are Jimmy Nicol, who filled in for an ailing Ringo during the band's 1964 international tour, and Neil Aspinall, the group's road manager, who, like George Martin, played a role in a few of the Beatles' recordings. Aspinall played a harmonica in the band's recording of "Being for the Benefit of Mr. Kite!" the tamboura on "Within You Without You," and percussion on the group's recording of "Magical Mystery Tour."

The nickname Fifth Beatle has also been given to two Americans. Pianist Billy Preston contributed his organ-playing to the recordings "Let It Be" and "I Want You" and played the electric piano on the recordings "Don't Let Me Down" and "Get Back." An African American, Preston has also been referred to as the Black Beatle. The New York disc jockey Murray the K, who was among the chief promoters of the group during their first appearances in America, actually made a point of calling himself the Fifth Beatle, and is, in fact, credited with having first used the term.

Billy Preston

The Beatles and their music still connect with their fans decades after the band broke up.

It's not only the kids. "I'd like to think," George said after his Beatles days were over, "that the old Beatles fans have grown up and they've got married and they've all got kids and they're all more responsible, but they still have a space in their hearts for us."

He would be more than gratified. Millions of old Beatles fans, now parents and grandparents, those who made Beatlemania one of history's greatest phenomena, have not only remained loyal fans, but have come to a deeper appreciation of how the Fab Four enriched their lives. The Beatles changed the world. They made it a better place in which to live. They were, in the words of their publicist Derek Taylor, "the twentieth century's greatest romance." Few would deny that it is a romance that has never ended.

BEATLES' US DISCOGRAPHY

(Singles that hit the Billboard Chart are indicated with their highest-ranking number in parentheses after song title. Number 1 hits appear in red.)

RELEASED	ALBUM TITLE	BILLBOARD RANK	RECORD LABEL
January 10, 1964	*Introducing the Beatles*	2	Vee-Jay

I Saw Her Standing There (14) • Misery • Anna (Go to Him) • Chains • Boys • Love Me Do (1) • P.S. I Love You (10) • Baby It's You (67) • Do You Want to Know a Secret (2) • A Taste of Honey • There's a Place (74) • Twist and Shout (2)

RELEASED	ALBUM TITLE	BILLBOARD RANK	RECORD LABEL
January 20, 1964	*Meet the Beatles!*	1	Capitol

I Want to Hold Your Hand (1) • I Saw Her Standing There (14) • This Boy • It Won't Be Long • All I've Got to Do • All My Loving (45) • Don't Bother Me • Little Child • Till There Was You • Hold Me Tight • I Wanna Be Your Man • Not a Second Time

RELEASED	ALBUM TITLE	BILLBOARD RANK	RECORD LABEL
April 10, 1964	*The Beatles' Second Album*	1	Capitol

Roll Over Beethoven (68) • Thank You Girl (35) • You Really Got a Hold on Me • Devil in Her Heart • Money (That's What I Want) • You Can't Do That (48) • Long Tall Sally • I Call Your Name • Please Mister Postman • I'll Get You • She Loves You (1)

RELEASED	ALBUM TITLE	BILLBOARD RANK	RECORD LABEL
June 26, 1964	*A Hard Day's Night*	1	United Artists

A Hard Day's Night (1) • Tell Me Why • I'll Cry Instead (25) • I'm Happy Just to Dance with You (95) • I Should Have Known Better (53) • If I Fell (53) • And I Love Her (12) • Can't Buy Me Love (1)

RELEASED	ALBUM TITLE	BILLBOARD RANK	RECORD LABEL
July 20, 1964	*Something New*	2	Capitol

I'll Cry Instead (25) • Things We Said Today • Any Time at All • When I Get Home • Slow Down (25) • Matchbox (17) • Tell Me Why • And I Love Her (12) • I'm Happy Just to Dance with You (95) • If I Fell (53) • Komm, Gib Mir Deine Hand

RELEASED	ALBUM TITLE	BILLBOARD RANK	RECORD LABEL
November 23, 1964	*The Beatles' Story*	7	Capitol

Interviews and snippets of previously released songs

RELEASED	ALBUM TITLE	BILLBOARD RANK	RECORD LABEL
December 15, 1964	*Beatles '65*	1	Capitol

No Reply • I'm a Loser • Baby's in Black • Rock and Roll Music • I'll Follow the Sun • Mr. Moonlight • Honey Don't • I'll Be Back • She's a Woman (4) • I Feel Fine (1) • Everybody's Trying to Be My Baby

RELEASED	ALBUM TITLE	BILLBOARD RANK	RECORD LABEL
March 22, 1965	*The Early Beatles*	43	Capitol

Love Me Do (1) • Twist and Shout (2) • Anna (Go to Him) • Chains • Boys • Ask Me Why • Please Please Me (3) • P.S. I Love You (10) • Baby It's You (67) • A Taste of Honey • Do You Want to Know a Secret (2)

RELEASED	ALBUM TITLE	BILLBOARD RANK	RECORD LABEL
June 14, 1965	*Beatles VI*	1	Capitol

Kansas City/Hey-Hey-Hey-Hey! • Eight Days a Week (1) • You Like Me Too Much • Bad Boy • I Don't Want to Spoil the Party (39) • Words of Love • What You're Doing • Yes It Is (46) • Dizzy Miss Lizzy • Tell Me What You See • Every Little Thing

RELEASED	ALBUM TITLE	BILLBOARD RANK	RECORD LABEL
August 13, 1965	*Help!*	1	Capitol

Help! (1) • The Night Before • You've Got to Hide Your Love Away • I Need You • Another Girl • Ticket to Ride (1) • You're Going to Lose That Girl

RELEASED	ALBUM TITLE	BILLBOARD RANK	RECORD LABEL
December 6, 1965	*Rubber Soul*	1	Capitol

I've Just Seen a Face • Norwegian Wood (This Bird Has Flown) • You Won't See Me • Think for Yourself • The Word • Michelle • It's Only Love • Girl • I'm Looking Through You • In My Life • Wait • Run for Your Life

RELEASED	ALBUM TITLE	BILLBOARD RANK	RECORD LABEL
June 20, 1966	*"Yesterday" . . . and Today*	1	Capitol

Drive My Car • I'm Only Sleeping • Nowhere Man (3) • Doctor Robert • Yesterday (1) • Act Naturally (47) • And Your Bird Can Sing • If I Needed Someone • We Can Work It Out (1) • What Goes On? (81) • Day Tripper (5)

RELEASED	ALBUM TITLE	BILLBOARD RANK	RECORD LABEL
August 8, 1966	*Revolver*	1	Capitol

Taxman • Eleanor Rigby (11) • Love You To • Here, There and Everywhere • Yellow Submarine (2) • She Said She Said • Good Day Sunshine • For No One • I Want to Tell You • Got to Get You into My Life (7) • Tomorrow Never Knows

RELEASED	ALBUM TITLE	BILLBOARD RANK	RECORD LABEL
June 2, 1967	*Sgt. Pepper's Lonely Hearts Club Band*	1	Capitol

Sgt. Pepper's Lonely Hearts Club Band (71) • With a Little Help from My Friends • Lucy in the Sky with Diamonds • Getting Better • Fixing a Hole • She's Leaving Home • Being for the Benefit of Mr. Kite! • Within You Without You • When I'm Sixty-Four • Lovely Rita • Good Morning Good Morning • Sgt. Pepper's Lonely Hearts Club Band (reprise) • A Day in the Life

RELEASED	ALBUM TITLE	BILLBOARD RANK	RECORD LABEL
November 27, 1967	*Magical Mystery Tour*	1	Capitol

Magical Mystery Tour • The Fool on the Hill • Flying • Blue Jay Way • Your Mother Should Know • I Am the Walrus (56) • Hello, Goodbye (1) • Strawberry Fields Forever (8) • Penny Lane (1) • Baby You're a Rich Man (34) • All You Need Is Love (1)

RELEASED	ALBUM TITLE	BILLBOARD RANK	RECORD LABEL
November 25, 1968	*The Beatles (White Album)*	1	Apple

Back in the U.S.S.R. • Dear Prudence • Glass Onion • Ob-La-Di, Ob-La-Da (49) • Wild Honey Pie • The Continuing Story of Bungalow Bill • While My Guitar Gently Weeps • Happiness Is a Warm Gun • Martha My Dear • I'm So Tired • Blackbird • Piggies • Rocky Raccoon • Don't Pass Me By • Why Don't We Do It in the Road? • I Will • Julia • Birthday • Yer Blues • Mother Nature's Son • Everybody's Got Something to Hide Except Me and My Monkey • Sexy Sadie • Helter Skelter • Long, Long, Long • Revolution I • Honey Pie • Savoy Truffle • Cry Baby Cry • Revolution 9 • Good Night

RELEASED	ALBUM TITLE	BILLBOARD RANK	RECORD LABEL
January 13, 1969	*Yellow Submarine*	2	Apple

Yellow Submarine (2) • Only a Northern Song • All Together Now • Hey Bulldog • It's All Too Much • All You Need Is Love (1)

RELEASED	ALBUM TITLE	BILLBOARD RANK	RECORD LABEL
October 1, 1969	*Abbey Road*	1	Apple

Come Together (1) • Something (1) • Maxwell's Silver Hammer • Oh! Darling • Octopus's Garden • I Want You (She's So Heavy) • Here Comes the Sun • Because • You Never Give Me Your Money • Sun King • Mean Mr. Mustard • Polythene Pam • She Came in Through the Bathroom Window • Golden Slumbers • Carry That Weight • The End • Her Majesty

RELEASED	ALBUM TITLE	BILLBOARD RANK	RECORD LABEL
February 26, 1970	*Hey Jude*	2	Apple

Can't Buy Me Love (1) • I Should Have Known Better (53) • Paperback Writer (1) • Rain (23) • Lady Madonna (4) • Revolution (12) • Hey Jude (1) • Old Brown Shoe • Don't Let Me Down (35) • The Ballad of John and Yoko (8)

RELEASED	ALBUM TITLE	BILLBOARD RANK	RECORD LABEL
May 18, 1970	*Let It Be*	1	Apple

Two of Us • Dig a Pony • Across the Universe • I Me Mine • Dig It • Let It Be (1) • Maggie Mae • I've Got a Feeling • One after 909 • The Long and Winding Road (1) • For You Blue (1) • Get Back (1)

HIT SINGLES THAT DIDN'T APPEAR ON A US ALBUM		
Original release: April 23, 1962 Reissued: January 27, 1964	"My Bonnie" (26)	Decca
Original release: May 27, 1963 Reissued: January 30, 1964	"From Me to You" (41)	Vee-Jay
May 21, 1964	"Sie Liebt Dich" (97)	Swan
March 18, 1968	"The Inner Light" (96)	Capitol

SOURCES

The following sources have been particularly important in presenting key concepts in this book

The books *Shout! The Beatles in Their Generation* by Philip Norman and *The Beatles* by Hunter Davies have become classic studies of the Fab Four. They provide detailed accounts of the Beatles from their beginnings until their breakup and include revealing anecdotes about John, Paul, George, and Ringo and the band as a whole.

The Beatles Anthology was an essential source in the preparation of this book. It contains hundreds of quotes from the Beatles themselves, providing essential insights into their experiences.

Bruce Spizer's *The Beatles Are Coming! The Birth of Beatlemania in America* was extremely important in supplying lively and detailed accounts of how, beginning with their first appearance on *The Ed Sullivan Show*, the Beatles conquered the United States and propelled Beatlemania into a worldwide phenomenon.

The *Rolling Stone* publication "The Beatles: The Ultimate Album-by-Album Guide" was particularly useful in detailing how the Beatles brought the way they revolutionized popular music to new and unprecedented heights once they stopped touring and retreated into the studio.

Yury Pelyushonok's *Strings for a Beatle Bass: The Beatles Generation in the USSR* was a vital and fascinating source of personal information about the remarkable ways in which the Beatles broke through the Iron Curtain and, against all odds, captured the hearts and minds of Russian youth.

FURTHER READING AND SURFING

PRINT

★ *Indicates books published specifically for young readers. All books are of interest to young readers.*
+ *Indicates significant source of quotations used in book*

+Beatles, The. *The Beatles Anthology.* San Francisco: Chronicle Books, 2002.

+"The Beatles: The Ultimate Album-by-Album Guide." Special issue, *Rolling Stone*, 2011.

+Davies, Hunter. *The Beatles.* New York: W. W. Norton, 2010.

★Edgers, Geoff. *Who Were the Beatles?* New York: Grosset & Dunlap, 2006.

★Gallagher, James. *The Beatles* (Pop Rock: Popular Rock Superstars of Yesterday and Today). Broomall, PA: Mason Crest Publishers, 2008.

Gladwell, Malcolm. *Outliers: The Story of Success.* Boston: Back Bay Books, 2011.

★Kallen, Stuart. *The Beatles* (Innovators). Farmington Hills, MI: Kidhaven Press, 2011.

Kane, Larry. *When They Were Boys: The True Story of the Beatles' Rise to the Top.* Philadelphia: Running Press, 2013.

★Kozinn, Allan. *The Beatles: From the Cavern to the Rooftop.* New York: Phaidon Press, 2010.

★Krull, Kathleen, Paul Brewer, illustrated by Stacy Innerst. *The Beatles Were Fab (and They Were Funny).* New York: Houghton Mifflin, 2013.

+Leigh, Spencer. *The Beatles in Hamburg: The Stories, the Scene and How It All Began.* Chicago: Chicago Review Press, 2011.

Leigh, Spencer. *The Beatles in Liverpool: The Stories, the Scene, and the Path to Stardom.* Chicago: Chicago Review Press, 2012.

+Norman, Philip. *Shout! The Beatles in Their Generation.* New York: Simon & Schuster, 2005.

★Partridge, Elizabeth. *John Lennon: All I Want Is the Truth.* New York: Viking, 2005.

Pelyushonok, Yury. *Strings for a Beatle Bass: The Beatles Generation in the USSR.* Self published, 2004.

★Roberts, Jeremy. *The Beatles: Musical Revolutionaries.* Minneapolis: Twenty-First Century Books, 2011.

Spitz, Bob. *The Beatles: The Biography.* Boston: Back Bay Books, 2006.

★Spitz, Bob. *Yeah! Yeah! Yeah! The Beatles, Beatlemania, and the Music That Changed the World.* New York: Little, Brown, 2007.

+Spizer, Bruce. *The Beatles Are Coming! The Birth of Beatlemania in America.* New Orleans: 498 Productions, 2010.

+Turner, Steve. *A Hard Day's Write: The Stories Behind Every Beatles Song.* New York: Harper Collins, 1994.

+★Wentzel, Jim. *The Beatles* (Rock & Roll Hall of Famers). New York: Rosen Publishing, 2001.

Woodhead, Leslie. *How the Beatles Rocked the Kremlin: The Untold Story of a Noisy Revolution.* New York: Bloomsbury, 2013.

INTERNET

Collectively, the websites listed below contain an extraordinary amount of information about the Beatles including profiles, sound clips of Beatles' songs, video clips of Beatles' performances, histories of the band, rare photographs, and much, much more.

www.thebeatles.com   www.beatlesagain.com   www.beatles-unlimited.com

www.merseybeat.ndo.co.uk   www.beatledrops.com   www.beatlesbible.com

www.beatlesmusic.pl   www.beatlelinks.net/links

INDEX

PHOTO CREDITS

ACKNOWLEDGMENTS

I am deeply indebted to Nancy Reyburn, Marie McHugh, Carol Sandler, and Ginger Mayo for the contributions they made to this book. A debt of gratitude is owed also to Ellice Lee and John Candell for their inspired design and to Sandy Smith and Ilana Worrell for so thoroughly checking the accuracy of every statement. I am most grateful for the assistance I received from Brooke Mason of Getty Images, Casey Anderson of Corbis Images, David Scripps and Simon Flavin at Mirrorpix, and Silka Quintero at the Granger Collection. I am particularly thankful for the continual help I received from Mary Kate Castellani. And once again it is essential that I acknowledge the fact that whatever magic this book may contain is due in greatest measure to the guidance and efforts of Emily Easton. Thank you, Emily.